Where Do You Stand?

Eight Moral Issues Confronting Today's Christians

Gregory C. Higgins

PAULIST PRESS
New York/Mahwah, N.J.

Library of Congress Cataloging-in-Publication Data

Higgins, Gregory C.,   1960-
    Where do you stand? : eight moral issues confronting today's Christians
/ Gregory C. Higgins.
      p.   cm.
    Includes bibliographical references.
    ISBN 0-8091-3608-2 (alk. paper)
    1. Christian ethics—Catholic authors. I. Title.
BJ1249.H54   1995   95-31454
241'.042—dc20   CIP

Published by Paulist Press
997 Macarthur Boulevard
Mahwah, NJ 07430

Printed and bound in the
United States of America

Contents

Preface

The goal of this book is a modest one. I felt there was a need to have a short book that could provide college students in introductory ethics courses and participants in parish study groups with a resource to assist them in their discussion of some of today's pressing ethical questions. The following chapters provide an overview of the key issues involved in the various ethical debates. College students may wish to read these chapters to prepare for upcoming class lectures or reading assignments. Depending on their schedule, a parish study group could select one or two issues for discussion during each of their meetings.

The scope of this investigation is deliberately limited. There are a number of very important pressing moral issues that are not discussed in the following pages. Such a limitation is, I hope, understandable. I have focused on what are often called "life issues." I have also limited the investigation to those issues about which either the Vatican or the National Conference of Catholic Bishops has issued some official teaching. This enables the readers to have a working knowledge of the church's positions on some of the most controversial issues of our time as well as an understanding of the reasoning used by church authorities in arriving at their moral positions. I intend this Catholic perspective to be an aid, not a hindrance, to this text's usefulness as a basis for ecumenical discussion.

In fairness to my readers two observations about the book should be made at the outset. First, the text proposes no solutions to the difficult ethical issues that will be discussed. I understand that this approach frustrates some readers, but I feel its merits outweigh its disadvantages. I believe that those who have little background in these matters benefit from first hearing both sides before having to take a stand on these ethical questions. In this way, readers are aware of the objections raised by each side while they reflect on the question. Second, I have deliberately chosen to minimize the discussion of a number of important theoretical aspects (e.g., freedom, conscience, sin) of ethics. I have tried to include a succinct account of those issues which are directly relevant for the discussion (e.g., the principle of double effect), but a fuller elaboration of these themes would certainly be needed in an academic setting. Readers wishing to pursue those areas in greater depth should consult the "suggested readings" at the end of each chapter.

In closing, I would like to thank a number of people. First, I need to thank my students who continue to teach me much more than they probably realize. Second, my colleagues at Christian Brothers Academy in Lincroft, NJ make it a pleasure to go to work each day. I thank them for that and much more. Thanks also to my colleagues at Brookdale Community College and Georgian Court College for allowing me to be part of their faculties. Third, I would like to thank Kevin Coyne, Joseph Incandela, and Fr. James Massa for reading the manuscript and offering their very helpful comments and suggestions. Finally, I would like to single out a number of people who are truly a blessing: Angela Higgins, James Higgins, J. Nolan Higgins, Chris Higgins, Jessica Higgins, Allison Higgins, and Eileen Higgins. It is to my wife Eileen that I lovingly dedicate this work.

Introduction

The goal of Christian ethical reflection is to determine proper and improper behavior for Christians.[1] Ethicists do not remain content to say how things *are*, but rather go beyond that to say how things *should* be. Citing an example from church history or the findings of an opinion poll may indeed prove illuminating in the course of ethical debate, but both of these sources leave unanswered the crucial ethical question about whether such events or beliefs should be praised or condemned. Should Christians have acted as they did, for example, during the Inquisition? Should Roman Catholics use artificial birth control? Opinion polls tell us what the majority thinks, but as history has shown, the majority is not always right. Making judgments about right and wrong is a difficult but necessary feature of Christian living, and it often generates a great deal of unrest within the Christian community.

This unrest arises in part because Christian ethical reflection involves the assigning and assuming of moral burdens. Christian belief makes demands upon those who profess it. We are commanded to take up the cross and follow Christ. Christian ethics, then, has as one of its tasks the identification of those burdens which Christians should rightfully assume. Is it morally permissible for Christians to enter into a second marriage if the first one fails? Is it morally permissible for a young Christian woman who discovers she is pregnant to have an abortion? Is it morally permissible for infertile Christians to have children through in *vitro* fertilization? The burdens we are asking others or ourselves to bear are often great. Such decisions require prayerful, thoughtful reflection and discussion.

This book focuses on many of the more dramatic ethical issues of our day. It is important for us to discuss these issues with our neighbors. Should we ever find ourselves facing decisions about such issues, this prior consideration may prove helpful at that critical time. This must not, however, overshadow the obvious fact that our lives are rarely a series of daily decisions of monumental proportions. Most of us, God willing, will not be confronted with the choice of whom to lock out of a fallout shelter before nuclear bombs annihilate our country. Rather, we spend the bulk of our time in our college years dealing with parents, siblings, roommates, and friends. In our adult years we associate most frequently with spouses, children, co-workers, friends, and neighbors. How we interact with our families, spouses, girlfriends or boyfriends, roommates, or those who serve us lunch in the dining hall provides a far more accurate benchmark of our morality than how we respond to the crises we only occasionally face.

Before we begin tackling specific moral questions, it will be necessary first to identify how we presently go about making moral decisions. We must then scrutinize this approach honestly. We need to ask the difficult questions: Do we use one type of argument for one issue, but reject that type of argument when discussing another issue? If we make exceptions to our rules, how do we justify them? How persuasive is an appeal to the Bible or to papal authority? These are but a few of the questions that will be raised in the following chapter.

Moral Reasoning

Faithful Christians do not always agree on how they should act. Some Christians support the death penalty, others do not. Some are pacifists; others favor military intervention in certain cases. Some would allow for homosexual activity; others think such activity is always wrong. How did this diversity of opinion arise? Part of the answer is that people go about their moral reasoning in different ways. Some place great emphasis on the Bible, others on their own conscience, still others on papal authority, to name but a few. Different people give greater weight to different sources of moral authority. Our study in Christian ethics, therefore, begins by identifying some of the ways by which people arrive at their moral positions.

In order to identify those reasons which you personally find morally persuasive, read the following situations and ask, "Is the behavior ethical?" Be sure to state as clearly as possible the reasons for your position. We need to identify and critique the ways in which we arrive at moral decisions since these approaches will be continually influencing the decisions we will be making throughout the course of our investigation.

Consider the following cases in terms of two questions: (a) Is the behavior ethical? and (b) Why? Why not?

1. In keeping with a time-honored religious tradition, Aztec priests sacrifice a child to their gods.

2. An unjust dictator attacks a neighboring nation which is an ally of the United States. The country under attack calls upon the U.S. for help and U.S. troops are sent into battle. The war initially goes poorly for the United States. At a critical moment in the fighting it is discovered through military intelligence that this dictator's only child is in a local hospital. The intelligence report offers a very high assurance that (a) the hospital wing in which the child is staying can be targeted and destroyed with relative ease and (b) that the death of the child will break the dictator psychologically and help the United States win the war quickly, with the result of fewer casualties on both sides. The U.S. decides to bomb the hospital, killing the dictator's child.

3. A homeless man steals bread and soup from a grocery during a riot in which looting is taking place.

4. Two mutually consenting adult men are involved in a long-standing monogamous homosexual relationship.

5. A devout Quaker punches a "loud mouth" who has ridiculed his religion.

6. A student enrolls in a college knowing that the school has an honor code which states, "I will not cheat or tolerate those who do." Students are required by the oath to report to the dean any incidents of cheating. This student sees another student who has been struggling academically cheating on the final exam. She does not report the incident.

7. A married Catholic couple has two children. After much

discussion, they mutually decide that for a variety of reasons, they would like to have no more children. The woman consults her physician and begins taking birth control pills.

Question #1: Are there objective moral truths?

The first situation involves the Aztec religious practice of sacrificing children. Our moral condemnation of that practice may take one of two forms. We may say, "Although they thought they were doing something proper, in fact they were wrong to kill children. The practice is immoral, period." The second response might be along the lines of, "While the practice is repugnant to us, who are we to judge? For them it was proper, for us it's improper." These two responses reflect two different understandings of morality. The first sees ethics as analogous to the physical sciences. Just as there are unchanging laws in physics, there exist certain moral laws which are similarly unalterable. Just as the denial of the existence of gravity does not make that force non-existent, the denial of the existence of moral truth does not mean such truths do not exist. While our understanding of right and wrong is greatly influenced by our upbringing, our culture, and our religion (to name but a few), there are certain actions that all rational persons know are immoral. Others disagree. The moral life in their view is analogous not to physics, but to cultural anthropology. The proper dress for a gentleman of the seventeenth century was a waistcoat and knee breeches. Today it is a three piece suit. Just as attitudes about clothing change with the times, so do attitudes about morality. Just as there is no one definitive version of "proper attire" for a gentleman, so too there is no one definitive account of moral right and wrong.

The first situation asks us to decide if we are "objectivists" or "relativists." The objectivist position is that moral truths are "objective" in that they exist apart from whether or not we acknowledge them. The refusal to believe in physical laws (e.g., the boiling point of water) does not change the fact that water boils at 212 degrees. In the same way, persons may say certain actions are morally acceptable, but that does not make them right in the eyes of the objectivist. These people are simply in error as was the person who doubted the existence of a boiling point. The relativists, by contrast, believe that an analogy from the physical sciences does not accurately reflect the situation in ethics. The wide diversity of moral codes as well as the rapid changes in our own cultural mores leads them to conclude that there is no one definitively correct moral code. Ethical judgments are always judgments *from a certain perspective*, with no one perspective necessarily any better than another.

Both approaches have their dangers. Objectivists must guard against intolerance. By seeing one and only one morally correct answer, they run the risk of failing to appreciate cultural diversity. The relativists, by contrast, run the risk of reducing all moral decisions to statements of preference rather than truth. Our moral protests and vehement debates are reduced to being the equivalent of arguing whether chocolate ice cream is better than vanilla ice cream.

Question #2: Are some actions always immoral to perform?

Ethics teachers are fond of creating hypothetical, often bizarre situations. Such exercises, however, often clarify crucial differences between rival ethical theories. The second situation is such an exercise. It leads us to ask, "Are there any actions which may never be performed? Are there any rules which may never be broken?" For purposes of illustrating the point, let us assume the following three ideas. First, the ally is being attacked unjustly. Second, the war is presently going poorly for the

United States. Third, the death of the dictator's only child will bring about a quick end to the war with fewer casualties on both sides. With those assumptions, let us review two responses to the question: Should we bomb the hospital?

There are a number of arguments commonly advanced to ethically justify such a bombing. For example, some would argue that in war there are no rules other than to win the war. Here, however, attention is focused on one particular response: We should bomb the hospital because in the long run we will save more lives. The death of the child is indeed tragic, but this death will result in an earlier conclusion to the war which means that hundreds or thousands of lives will be saved in the long run. In the ethical terminology of a group of ethicists known as utilitarians, dropping the bomb is justified because it results in "the greatest good for the greatest number." The reasoning here is very straightforward: compare the results of bombing the hospital against the results of not bombing the hospital and decide which will provide the better results. Bombing the hospital results in the unfortunate death of one child, but brings the war to a speedy close. Not bombing the hospital brings about continued human suffering and an increased death toll. Since the former set of results is ethically preferable to the latter, the bombing is an ethical act.

The reasoning used above focused on the consequences of bombing or not bombing the hospital. There are those, however, who do not consider consequences relevant to deciding the issue. For these thinkers, certain actions are wrong in and of themselves and could never be justified. In this case, the direct taking of the life of an innocent child is wrong. No matter how noble the results one seeks to achieve, the achievement of those goals through the direct taking of innocent human life is absolutely immoral. We may never choose to commit an intrinsically immoral act. We must do the right thing, not try to speculate on the possible results, which we often can not adequately judge. For example, members of a jury must render decisions purely on the basis of the facts presented in the case. They should not concern themselves with how their verdicts will influence society. They must do their duty as jurors to render a fair and impartial decision and nothing else.

The debate boils down to two different understandings of moral rules. Utilitarians regard rules as valuable, yet dispensable moral guidelines. Rules represent the sum total of our collective moral wisdom, but they can never cover every situation and must be broken if they prevent the greatest good for the greatest number from being achieved. Others maintain that certain actions are immoral by their very nature and consequently can never be justified. Certain prohibitions (e.g., "do not rape," "do not kill the innocent") are absolutely inviolable. Critics of utilitarianism fear that without such absolute prohibitions, people can justify any number of immoral actions by appealing to some "greater good."

Question #3: If rules may be broken, how are legitimate exceptions determined?

The third situation of the homeless man stealing bread and soup follows from the second situation in that it puts the focus on the status of rules in the moral life. For some the prohibition against stealing is absolute. All forms of stealing are wrong, and if we begin to justify such violations of basic moral codes we will completely undermine the ethical life. In this third situation, however, we examine the response which regards stealing as being wrong in most cases, but is willing to recognize a certain limited number of cases as being exceptions to the rule. Here one weighs the rule against the circumstance in which the rule is broken. If the situation is desperate enough, then the rule may be violated. We need to examine more closely the steps involved in making such a determination.

The circumstances surrounding an act greatly influence our moral evaluation. For example, we recognize the ethical difference between first degree murder and killing in self-defense. Although both actions result in the death of another human being, we offer different moral evaluations of them. In a more formal way, let us analyze the manner in which that distinction is made. First, a rule or principle is identified: Do not kill. Second, exceptions to that rule are listed. A common exception to that rule is the protection of innocent third parties from an unjust aggressor. If a crazed gunman is about to kill an innocent child and I have the opportunity to stop that person by violent means, even lethal means, then I may ethically perform that action. Another commonly held exception is self-defense. There are other exceptions, and it should be noted that some people would reject the two exceptions already given. The third step in this process of moral reasoning is to examine the particular situation. Did the person kill the other person in defense of an innocent third party or in self-defense? If the person's action is deemed to be one of the actions which are considered valid exceptions to the rule, then the behavior was morally acceptable. If the person's action is not deemed to be one of the actions that are considered valid exceptions, then the behavior was immoral. Did the person have, for example, a way of stopping the attacker without having to actually kill the person? This process may seem abstract, but it is precisely this process that a jury often follows in its deliberations. They must hear testimony, weigh the various arguments, and reach a decision as to the guilt or innocence of the person.

Difficulties arise in two areas. First, which exceptions will be allowed? Does the prohibition against killing apply to animals, as animal rights activists claim? Second, how can we know the inner disposition of another human being?

Motivation is frequently a factor in the list of exceptions, but how can we know what is in another's heart? Supporters, however, insist that this approach preserves the commitment to rules while allowing for flexibility which is necessary when dealing with the moral ambiguities of human existence.

Question #4: What role should the Bible play in our moral reflection?

The fourth situation of the homosexual couple actually highlights two traditional areas of moral guidance. The first has been and continues to be one of the most important and influential sources for Christians when making an ethical decision: the Bible. Traditional opposition to homosexual activity is based in part on scriptural passages such as:

> Now we know that the law is good, provided that one uses it as law, with the understanding that law is meant not for a righteous person but for the lawless and unruly, the godless and sinful, the unholy and profane, those who kill their fathers or mothers, murderers, the unchaste, practicing homosexuals, kidnapers, liars, perjurers, and whatever else is opposed to sound teaching, according to the glorious gospel of the blessed God, with which I have been entrusted (1 Tim 1:8–11).

Many Christians regard passages such as these as binding teaching on all Christians. The author of 1 Timothy condemns "practicing homosexuals," and lists them among others whose activity is contrary to "sound teaching" and not in accordance with the "glorious gospel of the blessed God."

The use of scripture raises a number of questions. Without attempting to deal with them all, two will be highlighted for our consideration. First, to what extent do you believe the scriptures reflect the times in which they were written as opposed to being the eternal word of God? The answer to this question directly impacts the degree to which we perceive the Bible as a trustworthy guide in making moral decisions. If we view the Bible as a reflection of a time gone by, then it serves little use for us now. If it reflects the eternal word of God, it is eminently relevant for us. If you fall somewhere in between, toward which side do you lean? Second, is there an overriding theme or set of themes against which scriptural appeals are measured? For example, those who maintain that the universal love of God is one of the central themes of the Bible would most likely qualify in some way those biblical verses that suggest that those who do not confess Jesus as Lord will be condemned.

Question #5: Are certain actions unnatural?

Christians have often advanced "natural law" arguments in their moral deliberations. In terms of the example of the homosexual couple, a natural law ethicist might argue that natural sexual inclination should be directed toward members of the opposite sex; consequently, homosexual orientation is distorted, and acting on these inclinations would be immoral. The central claim of natural law ethicists is that despite outward differences in terms of size, shape, color, etc., all humans share a common human nature. Natural law ethicists would argue that it is in our very nature to want to acquire knowledge, to establish a just society, and to have a family. These tendencies are innate, not learned. All humans, in other words, share certain goals and usually act in ways which bring them closer to achieving those goals.

These built-in goals or purposes of human activity are then used to offer moral evaluations of human behavior. For example, all humans, it is claimed, have a natural drive toward self-preservation. We would consider it odd if someone's head were held under water and that person did not respond or try in any way to break free. The "natural" thing to do would be to struggle and fight to survive. Since we are created by God, the Christian tradition has looked upon these natural inclinations as God-given. Therefore, the equation has been made between "unnatural" and "sinful" acts. In a natural law perspective, suicide is wrong because it is both unnatural (a violation of the natural drive toward self-preservation) and sinful (a violation of the commandment against murder).

The natural law tradition recognizes that people perform unnatural actions. Persons may either lack the full capacity (e.g., mental illness) to understand the natural law or they may know the action is unnatural but simply choose to perform the action anyway. To natural law ethicists reason should be the main arbiter of which inclinations should be acted upon and which should not. Humans are filled with all kinds of inclinations, but if we wish to live a moral life we should not act on all of them. Those who lack sufficient use of reason, therefore, may unknowingly perform immoral actions. Equal emphasis is placed on the human ability to knowingly act immorally. Knowing the natural law does not force the person to act in accordance with it. Human free will allows persons to perform great acts of human goodness or horrible acts of evil and accept responsibility for their actions.

Critics have charged that appeals to what is "natural" behavior too often became equated with what is "socially accepted" behavior. Appeals to natural law, therefore, disguise certain prejudices. Claims have been made, for example, that racial segregation was ordained by nature or that "the woman's (natural) place was in the home." Supporters, on the other hand, insist that the natural law follows logically from the Christian belief that all humans are created in the image and likeness of God. Human rights, they argue, depend on the existence of the natural law, since humans are not "given" such rights by any government, but rather are endowed with them by the creator.

Question #6: What qualities should Christians exhibit in their behavior?

Those in the natural law tradition insist that all persons, through use of their reason, would agree that we should "do the good and avoid evil." While certainly abstract, this claim would nonetheless receive universal agreement. It leaves unanswered, of course, the question of what constitutes "the good" to be pursued, and "the evil" to be avoided. Because of this, the natural law tradition has historically included in its understanding of the moral life a treatment of the virtues. The Greek word "arete," which we translate as "virtue," means excellence or skill. Simply put, a virtue is a skill that helps us to live moral lives. To say that we should be "good people" is not enough; we need to learn what skills or qualities a "good person" should have. In the cases of the Quaker who acted violently and the student who has taken an oath to uphold the honor code, virtues figure prominently in the evaluation of their behavior. Quakers have directly linked their identity as a religious group with a deep commitment to the virtue of peacefulness. The student who has taken an oath to uphold the honor code must consider her integrity when deciding whether to report the incident or not.

Virtues are the qualities which help us develop into the type of people we want to become. For example, suppose a college undergraduate was planning to go to medical school to become a doctor. Obviously this student wants to be a "good doctor." But what does that mean? To be a "good doctor" necessarily entails the cultivation of certain skills. The doctor must possess a superior knowledge of illnesses, their causes, and their cures. It also means, however, that he or she should be able to comfort the sick, listen attentively to their concerns, respond to their questions respectfully, and be willing to speak truthfully to them without being cold or distant.

The Greeks spoke of prudence, temperance, fortitude, and justice as the four "cardinal virtues" since the moral life hinged on the successful appropriation of those qualities or skills. For example, suppose a student has failed a course. The teacher must accomplish a goal: informing the student of a failing grade. However, the manner in which this is done is vital to the on-going academic life of the student. If a student is lazy, the teacher should be forceful and demanding. If the student is working to the best of his or her abilities, the teacher should be encouraging and supportive. If the teacher misreads the situation and informs the student in an inappropriate way, the teacher may have done more harm than good. The ability to know how to deal with individual students is a skill that must be developed over the course of a teaching career. At a certain point, such behavior becomes "second nature" to the teacher.

Those favoring a rules approach to ethics believe that an appeal to virtues does not offer sufficient moral guidance. Saying that a person should be a "good doctor" is too general an admonition and does not provide specific guidance when confronting a moral decision. They insist that rules are needed to help a caring doctor decide, for example, if it is morally permissible to lie to a patient about his or her condition. A second problem arises when the virtues conflict. When determining punishment many people feel torn between justice and mercy. They want to be both just and merciful since they value both qualities, yet frequently justice and mercy lead to different decisions.

A discussion of virtues asks us to decide an important question: Are the ethical conclusions meant to persuade all people or only those who profess Christian belief? Those who argue the former contend that such an approach is absolutely necessary in societies such as our own with a high degree of diversity. Frequently appealing to the natural law, these participants in the public debate wish to emphasize that which is common to both Christians and non-Christians. Those emphasizing a virtues approach wish to preserve the distinctive voice of Christianity in society and tend to frame their arguments in ways which emphasize the specifically Christian perspective on a given moral issue.

Question #7: What authority does the church have in our moral decisions?

One final area concerns us. In 1968 Pope Paul VI issued an encyclical letter entitled *Humanae Vitae* in which he set forth official Catholic teaching regarding artificial birth control. In essence, the pope made a natural law argument. When a married couple acts in accordance with the natural rhythms in a woman's reproductive cycle by abstaining from sexual relations during times of greater likelihood of fertility, the couple is acting morally since such actions are in accordance with the natural laws established by God. When, however, one artificially prevents ovulation or conception, then the person is acting outside the moral limits established by the creator. No one is morally entitled to break the natural, divinely-willed connection between the union of husband and wife and procreation.

The question concerning us at the present moment is not the argument itself, but rather the obligation of Catholics to live by such teachings. How much weight should Catholics give to papal teaching? On the one hand, some argue that membership in the church carries with it a moral obligation to abide by the teaching of the leader of the church. For others, the papal teaching must be weighed against other considerations; if a Catholic chooses to follow a course of action which is contrary to the pope's teaching, then such dissent must be respected. The former group is concerned about "cafeteria Catholics," that is, church members who choose their beliefs the way cafeteria patrons choose their dinners, selecting only those items they find appealing. The latter group fears that the church would become a group of "robotic Catholics" who accept what they are told without critically examining the teaching. The former group highlights the need for unity in the church; the latter group insists that the church needs to subject its teachings to critical examination. Whether dissent is allowed, and, if so, at which points, continues to be debated with the church.

Discussion Questions

1. How do you go about making a moral decision?
2. Do you believe that "objective moral truth" exists?
3. Is it ever morally permissible to kill the innocent?
4. Do you accept or reject the idea that a "natural law" exists?
5. Does the Bible reflect the will of God or the culture in which it was produced?
6. What qualities are essential to Christian living?
7. Is it possible for someone to live in a way contrary to church teaching and still be "a good Catholic"?

Suggested Readings

For a recent official church teaching on the moral life, see *Veritatis Splendor* (*The Splendor of Truth*) by Pope John Paul II (Washington, D.C.: United States Catholic Conference, 1993). and *Evangelicum Vitae* (The Gospel of Life) by Pope John Paul II (Washington, D.C.: United States Catholic Conference, 1995). Section four of chapter two deals directly with the issue of objective moral truth. For an exposition of many of the fundamental themes in Catholic moral thought, see part one of the Vatican II constitution Gaudium et Spes ("Pastoral Constitution on the Church in the Modern World") in *Documents of Vatican II* (Grand Rapids: William B. Eerdmans Publishing Company, 1975), edited by Austin P. Flannery.

For a fuller exposition of themes in Catholic moral theology see *Reason Informed by Faith: Foundations of Catholic Morality* by Richard M. Gula, S.S. (Mahwah: Paulist Press, 1989) and *Principles for a Catholic Morality* by Timothy E. O'Connell, Revised Edition (San Francisco: Harper-Collins, 1990). For an exposition and defense of traditional methods and conclusions, see David Bohr, *Catholic Moral Tradition: In Christ, A New Creation* (Huntington: Our Sunday Visitor Publishing, 1990).

Reproductive Technology

Review the following cases. Are these actions justified or unjustified? Why?

1. A single woman has devoted herself to her career and by age thirty-five has become financially secure. She feels at this point in her life that she would like to leave the business world and start a family. She is currently not involved with a man, so she decides to be artificially inseminated at a sperm bank.

2. In order to make a little money, a college student sells his sperm to a sperm bank.

3. A couple is trying desperately to start a family when the husband discovers that he is sterile. His wife asks him if he would consider the possibility of her going to a sperm bank to be artificially inseminated. At first, he refuses to consider the possibility. Weeks later he tells his wife, "I want very much to have a family with you, but in all honesty, seeing my wife carrying a baby I know isn't mine will be difficult for me at times to handle. But I know that's just my pride speaking, so let's go ahead and follow your suggestion." She becomes artificially inseminated.

4. A monogamous lesbian couple involved in a long-standing relationship decide to have a child. One of the women is artificially inseminated.

5. Fearing that exposure to chemical warfare might leave him sterile, a soldier deposits his sperm in a sperm bank before leaving for a war. Tragically, he is killed in the war. His widow becomes artificially inseminated with her deceased husband's sperm.

6. A woman agrees to be a surrogate mother for a married couple. She has two children of her own and has been a surrogate mother once. She signs an agreement stating that she will not form a maternal bond with the child, but at the birth of the child she feels she can not surrender the child. She begins legal proceedings to keep the baby.

The following have to do with in vitro fertilization. If you are unfamiliar with this procedure, return to these questions after reading the chapter.

7. A married couple is unable to have children because the wife has blocked fallopian tubes. The couple decides to have a child through in vitro fertilization.

8. A wife has a medical condition which triples her chances for having a miscarriage. She has already experienced one miscarriage and fears she will have another. She and her husband enroll in an in vitro program, but hire a woman to be the "carrier" of the fertilized eggs.

9. A married couple enrolls in an in vitro program. Seven eggs are fertilized. Four are returned to the woman and two implant. The three remaining embryos are frozen. The couple has determined that they would only want two children. They donate the three embryos to an

institute for genetic research for its experiments to determine the cause of certain genetic diseases.

10. A petite woman enrolls in an in vitro program. Four eggs are fertilized and returned to the woman. All four implant. The doctor doesn't think she is physically capable of bringing four children to full term and fears she might miscarry or deliver extremely premature children. When the woman is one month pregnant, the doctor recommends that she undergo a procedure in which two of the four fertilized eggs will be removed. She agrees to the procedure.

For a variety of reasons, couples are not always able to have children. For many this is an excruciatingly painful problem, but it is also a problem that can be remedied by certain modern medical technologies. "Reproductive technology" includes a range of medical procedures that have human conception as their common goal. While this technology does exist and in fact has proven effective, the ethical question remains: Should infertile couples (or others) avail themselves of such reproductive technologies? We will focus primarily on two of the reproductive technologies currently available: artificial insemination and in *vitro* fertilization.

Before reviewing the specific procedures involved in this area, a brief word needs to be made about why this issue begins our study. First, a discussion of reproductive technology serves as a logical starting point for a study in "life issues" since here we are dealing with the beginning of life. Second, an investigation into this issue will, I believe, give us some appreciation of the complexity of certain moral issues, especially those involving modern medical technology. Finally, for many people this area of medical technology remains a mystery; therefore, many people have not formed deeply felt convictions about the morality or immorality of certain procedures. As such, it serves as a good testing ground for many of the theoretical issues we reviewed in the previous chapter. From here on, we need to apply those theoretical considerations to actual moral problems. If the starting point were abortion, for example, the examination of those theoretical issues might well be overshadowed by a concentration on the conclusions themselves, rather than on the method by which one arrived at those positions.

Artificial Insemination

We begin with artificial insemination. Artificial insemination (AI) is the most widely used reproduction-aiding technology today. In this procedure semen is collected and mechanically introduced into the woman's reproductive tract.[1] If the semen is taken from the woman's husband, the procedure is designated AIH (artificial insemination by a husband). If the semen is from a man not her husband, the procedure is designated AID (artificial insemination by a donor). AIH is used when a husband may not be able to perform sexually, but the couple wishes to have a child. A married couple may elect AID if they run a high risk of conceiving a child with certain genetic disorders. A single woman may wish to have a child and go to a sperm bank to be artificially inseminated.

Each form of artificial insemination raises its own set of questions. Catholic moral theologians have debated the morality of the various means of obtaining semen from the husband.[2] In terms of AID, some moral theologians are concerned that in the case of a married couple, the introduction of a third party into the act of procreation violates the marriage vows. In the case of the single woman, critics charge that it is unfair to bring a child into this world who has no possibility of knowing his or her father. There is also the very practical difficulty of the children being deprived of information concerning their medical histories which may be important later in their lives. Ethical concerns have also been raised about the activity of the donor: Is it ethical to donate or sell sperm that will be used to bring into the world a child you will never know? One final consideration may strike many as utterly incredible, except for the fact that it has already happened. One donor may actually be the biological father of any number of children. In one celebrated case, an inseminating physician used his own sperm to artificially inseminate his patients. This raises the possibility of half brothers and sisters unknowingly marrying one another at some later date.

AID has made possible the practice of surrogate motherhood in which a woman (commonly referred to as "the surrogate mother") is artificially inseminated and agrees upon the birth of the child to surrender the baby to the donor and his wife. The most celebrated case of this involved Mary Beth Whitehead. In such arrangements the possibility for ethical, emotional, and legal entanglements multiply. On the ethical front, those who oppose the practice contend that this entire process reduces human life to a commodity to be manufactured and purchased. This could also lead to the exploitation of poorer women. Others believe that such arrangements overlook the emotional bond formed by the woman to her baby during the nine months of pregnancy. Legal experts debate the legality of such contracts. Does this practice amount to baby selling? If so, a contract for an illegal activity has no legally binding power and, as such, these surrogacy agreements would have no legal standing.

In Vitro Fertilization

The second reproductive technology we will explore is *in vitro* fertilization. "*In vitro*" conception takes place "in glass" (i.e., in a petri dish). The first in *vitro* baby (commonly referred to as "the first 'test tube baby' ") was Louise Brown, born July 26, 1978 in England. In this procedure, a woman is given a drug to stimulate her ovaries to produce multiple eggs. These eggs are then surgically removed. The eggs are co-incubated with sperm for around 12–18 hours to allow fertilization to take place. After 48–72 hours the embryo[3] is transferred to the uterine cavity by a catheter. If successful, implantation in the uterus will occur in two to three days.[4] In cases of women with blocked fallopian tubes or men with low sperm counts, the procedure offers them a greater chance of conceiving a child.

IVF generates a possibility for seemingly endless combinations of persons involved in the birth of a child. IVF may involve more parties than simply a husband and wife. It is possible to have donors of either eggs, sperm, or embryos. It is possible to have carriers who are not genetically related to the child. For example, it is theoretically possible to have five people involved in the birth process: the woman who donates her eggs, the man who donates his sperm, the woman who volunteers to carry the child to term, and the husband and wife who will adopt the child.

The entire cycle is physically, emotionally, and financially draining. The woman must undergo hormone treatment first for the purpose of producing eggs and then for optimizing the chances for the implantation of the fertilized eggs in the uterus. This may involve daily injections. Some critics fear that this hormonal treatment may increase a woman's chances for ovarian cancer. Heartbreak and desperation loom on the horizon for many since most experts put the success rate at between 15% and 20% for all women beginning an IVF cycle. Costing several thousands of dollars per attempt, IVF is an expensive procedure that is often not covered by a patient's medical insurance.

Because the IVF procedure is so demanding physically and emotionally, many IVF clinics have developed certain practices intended to help reduce the number of attempts a woman would have to make at IVF. A typical example might be as follows. A doctor is able to harvest six eggs from the woman and five are fertilized in the petri dish. The doctor returns three fertilized eggs to the woman. This involves a bit of "playing the odds" with nature. A doctor would return three fertilized eggs in the hope that one or two will implant. In some cases, all the fertilized eggs implant. In that case, we discover one of the many points at which this debate intersects with the abortion debate. The IVF procedure rarely involves the fertilization and return of a single egg. That would make the process much lengthier, costlier, more physically demanding, and much less successful.

The fertilization of many eggs, however, raises a number of ethical questions. It should be noted that not all IVF clinics freeze embryos; some clinics fertilize only a certain number of eggs and return all the fertilized eggs to the woman. The practice of freezing embryos is, however, not uncommon. If five eggs are fertilized and only three are returned to the woman, the two remaining fertilized eggs may be frozen. If none of the three eggs implant, these two fertilized eggs are available for transfer to the woman without her having to go through another IVF cycle. A number of concerns have been raised about this aspect of the IVF process. First, the thawing process is not without its perils. Richard McCormick reports that 30–40% of the eggs routinely do not survive the thawing process. Do these odds render the practice of freezing fertilized eggs immoral? Second, suppose two of the three eggs implant and the woman gives birth to two healthy children and the couple decides not to have any more children. What happens to the two frozen fertilized eggs? Could they be used in research? Could they be destroyed? It is on the question of the status of the frozen embryos that one sees a direct link between the debates over reproductive technologies and abortion.

The Vatican Instruction Regarding Reproductive Technology

In 1987 the Congregation for the Doctrine of the Faith, headed by Cardinal Joseph Ratzinger issued the *Instruction on Respect for Human Life in Its Origin and on the Dignity of Procreation.*[5] This document directly addresses the ethics of the various forms of reproductive technology. The Instruction bases its conclusions on a number of principles. One of these principles is that the only ethically appropriate context for procreation is marriage. A second principle, closely related to the first, is that conception must involve only the husband and wife. AID and IVF involving third parties (the Instruction refers to these as "heterologous artificial fertilization") are "contrary to the unity of marriage, to the dignity of the spouses, to the vocation proper to parents, and to the child's right to be conceived and brought into the world in marriage and from marriage."[6] These two principles exclude the involvement of any third parties in the conception and birth of children. What about those techniques which involve only a husband and wife?

The Instruction places a great deal of weight on the following principle: There exists a necessary connection between the unitive and the procreative meaning of the conjugal act. This terminology is dense and requires clarification. The Instruction insists that the sexual union of husband and wife (i.e., "the unitive meaning") must necessarily be joined to their openness to bringing new life into the world (i.e., "the procreative meaning"). In other words, there exists an inseparable connection between love-making and life-giving. AIH and IVF are procreative, but not physically unitive. While this does not exclude all possible methods of AIH, it does exclude IVF since in that procedure conception takes place outside the body.[7] This principle also underlies the teaching regarding artificial birth control. Artificial birth control technologically renders the sexual relations of husband and wife unitive, but not procreative. *In vitro* fertilization renders the couple procreative, but the act is not unitive.

The reasoning employed in the Instruction and the conclusions drawn from that reasoning have, of course, stirred great debate.[8] In terms of the reasoning, some have argued that the Instruction moves too quickly from saying that these are *unusual* (or perhaps *unnatural*) ways to have children to saying that they are *immoral* ways to have children. Pursuing that line of reasoning, critics charge, we would have to condemn the use of kidney dialysis, a medical technology that artificially mimics the natural functions of the kidneys. Those who defend the reasoning in the Instruction insist that such criticism is misplaced. The Instruction states, "These interventions are not rejected on the grounds that they are artificial. As such, they bear witness to the possibilities of the art of medicine. But they must be given a moral evaluation in reference to the dignity of the human person, who is called to realize his vocation from God to the gift of love and the gift of life."[9] These technological interventions, in other words, are not rejected because they are artificial, but because they go beyond the moral limits set by the creator. Others agree with the basic approach but arrive at different conclusions. One could agree that there is a necessary connection between union and procreation in marriage without necessarily condemning all instances of *in vitro* fertilization. The commitment of the married couple to the *in vitro* process testifies to their commitment to one another and to their openness to new life. In other words, the use of *in vitro* fertilization may not necessarily break the connection between love and life. Others see great wisdom in the ethical warnings found in the Instruction. Of particular concern is the potential disregard for the embryo: The Instruction devotes an entire section to "Respect for Human Embryos." Archbishop Daniel Pilarczyk writes: "The fundamental insight [of the document] is: Human life is precious, human life has a particular dignity, a particular sacredness because it is God's gift—a gift in its origin, a gift in its development, a gift in its ultimate destiny.... In short, human life is not a product to be manufactured as needed; human beings are not animals to be bred according to given specifications. All is quite logical, if one accepts the premise."[10]

Before concluding, it is interesting to examine the ways in which arguments are advanced in the Instruction. For example, although the positions in the Instruction are rooted in a biblical understanding of marriage and family, there are few direct quotations from the Bible. Neither does the Instruction look only at results. That is, the Instruction does not say, "Since having a child is a beautiful thing, any procedure which results in the birth of a child must be moral." There are many ways of having children that the Instruction regards as ethically unacceptable. The Instruction argues most frequently in terms of principles. These principles grow out of the church's understanding of the nature of procreation, but their validity, it is argued, does not depend on religious belief. Cardinal Ratzinger urges governments to enact laws prohibiting, among other things, surrogate motherhood. When we step back and analyze an ethical position, we begin to weigh the various arguments and counter-arguments. At that point, we can begin to see how those theoretical issues we discussed in the first chapter impact our own moral reasoning. Applying that more specifically to the Instruction, do you accept the reasoning used in the Instruction? Do you agree or disagree with the conclusions? Are there counter-arguments you find more persuasive?

How should single or married Christians respond to their desire to have children in face of their current inability to do so? For single women, this raises the question of the morality of artificial insemination. For married couples this might well raise the question of the morality of *in vitro* fertilization. Is adoption a better course of action for childless couples than medical technology? The issues seem overwhelming, but surrendering ourselves to silence is not a real option for most concerned Christians. Despite the complexity of the issues, discussion must continue, since with these technologies we are dealing with the very origin of human life.

Discussion Questions

1. Do you personally find the following morally acceptable or unacceptable: AIH, AID, surrogate motherhood, IVF between a husband and a wife, IVF involving third parties?
2. Does every woman have a *right* to have a child?
3. Do you agree with the reasoning which is employed in the Instruction? Do you accept or reject the conclusions of the Instruction?

Suggested Readings

The official church teaching can be found in the *Instruction on Respect for Human Life in Its Origin and on the Dignity of Procreation: Replies to Certain Questions of the Day* (Washington, D.C.: United States Catholic Conference, 1987).

A very helpful introduction to the question can be found in Richard McCormick, S.J.'s "Therapy or Tampering? The Ethics of Reproductive Technology," in *America* December 7,

1985. This essay is reprinted in a slightly modified form as chapter nineteen in McCormick's *The Critical Calling: Reflections on Moral Dilemmas Since Vatican II* (Washington, D.C.: Georgetown University Press, 1989).

The entry "Reproductive Technologies" by John C. Fletcher in the *Westminster Dictionary of Christian Ethics* is also very useful.

For an excellent critical review of the Instruction, see Edward V. Vacek, S.J.'s "Notes on Moral Theology," in *Theological Studies* (49) 1988, pp. 110–131.

Theology students would benefit from the following book length discussions of the issue: *The Ethics of Reproductive Technology* , edited by Kenneth D. Alpern (Oxford: Oxford University Press, 1992) and *Religion and Artificial Reproduction* by Thomas A. Shannon and Lisa Sowle Cahill (New York: Crossroad, 1988).

Abortion
〜〜〜〜〜〜〜〜

Review the following cases. Would abortion be justified or not?

1. A sexually active couple in college use birth control on an inconsistent basis.

Both are in their junior year in college when they conceive a child. The man suggests they marry, yet the woman feels unprepared to assume the duties of parenthood and marriage. She especially fears how her parents would react to news of her pregnancy.

2. A married couple feel they can't support any more children, so the husband has a vasectomy. A few months later, his wife discovers she is pregnant. It is discovered that the husband's vasectomy was improperly performed. She is one month pregnant.

3. During her fifth month of pregnancy, a woman learns that she has a high probability of delivering a child with Down's syndrome. The degree to which the child will be afflicted with Down's syndrome is not able to be determined.

4. Bitter ethnic rivalries result in civil war. One ethnic group rapes women captured in attacks on the communities of

rival forces. Ethnic purity is highly valued. Children born from these acts of violence are socially ostracized. A rape victim seeks an abortion after she learns she is one month pregnant.

5. A nation is highly populated and living on a very limited land mass. The government mandates that each married couple can have two children. Should a woman become pregnant with a third child, the woman must have an abortion.

Are these actions justified or unjustified?

6. A recently divorced woman has a "one-night stand" with an old friend. The next day she realizes she is midway through her cycle and decides to take a pill which will prevent the implantation of any fertilized egg in the uterine wall.

7. A Catholic governor personally opposes abortion but signs legislation approving abortion funding.

8. A politician introduces legislation that would prohibit the use of Medicaid funds for abortions.

9. A fourteen year old girl is sexually active. After learning she is pregnant, she has an abortion without being required to get parental consent.

10. Members of a radical pro-life organization bomb an abortion clinic at night.

Abortion reigns as the most hotly debated ethical issue in America today. On January 22, 1973 the United States Supreme Court handed down its ruling in the case of a Texas woman named in court documents as "Jane Roe." She had sought to have an abortion at a time when Texas state law prohibited abortions, except in cases to save the life of the mother. The court held in the *Roe v. Wade* decision that the constitutional right to privacy guaranteed a woman's right to have an abortion during the first trimester (i.e., the first three months of pregnancy). During the second trimester of pregnancy the state "may, if it chooses, regulate the abortion procedure in ways that are reasonably related to maternal health."[1] Only in the third trimester may the state constitutionally prohibit abortions, except to preserve the life or health of the mother. In the words of the court: "The State in promoting its interest in the potentiality of human life may, if it chooses, regulate, and even proscribe, abortion except where it is necessary, in appropriate medical judgment, for the preservation of the life or health of the mother."[2] This decision ignited a fire storm of debate across America that continues to the present day. We turn first to those who reject the court's decision.

The Pro-Life Position

The pro-life position, simply stated, is as follows:

(i)   Life (or personhood) begins at conception.[3]
(ii) The direct taking of innocent human life is always wrong.
(iii) From the moment of conception there is innocent human life.
(iv) Therefore, direct abortions are always immoral.

The abortion debate revolves around the first two premises. The pro-life advocates insist that life (or personhood) begins at the moment of conception and that the direct taking of that innocent human life is always wrong. The third premise is basically a restatement of the first two. The abortion debate, for all of its apparent complexity, amounts to a battle over the truth of those two claims.

The pro-life position concludes with a prohibition against "direct abortions." In order to understand fully this conclusion, we need to review a rather technical issue in moral theology. Before turning to that technical discussion, let us consider a hypothetical case. Suppose a husband and wife have a little boy who is both blind and deaf. Imagine further that this small child wanders into the street and does not notice a speeding car coming up behind him on the road. The boy's father, seeing his boy in this life-threatening situation, runs into the street and pushes the boy out of harm's way, but is himself struck and killed by the motorist. Ignore for now the important point that the father seems to be acting on instinct or emotion rather than on reason or conscious deliberation. Did the father do the right thing? If he did not act, his son would be killed; but by acting, the father lost his own life.

Moral theologians recognized long ago that life sometimes presents us with situations in which one action will produce two results, one good and one bad. Moral theologians refer to this as a "double effect." The moral question is, "May I ethically go ahead and perform the action knowing that this bad result will occur?" Slowly a consensus developed in Roman Catholic moral theology that a person may go ahead and perform the action if certain conditions were met. Andrew Varga offers the following as a summary of the traditional conditions which need to be met:[4]

(1) The act we intend to perform is good or at least indifferent by nature.
(2) The good and bad effects follow simultaneously from the act.
(3) One only intends the good effect and merely tolerates the undesired bad effect.
(4) The good effect outweighs the bad effect, or at least

there is proportionately grave reason for permitting the evil effect.

Each of these conditions requires a bit of explanation. The first specifies that the act to be performed is not an evil act (e.g., adultery). The second condition further restricts our consideration to those cases where one action produces two effects *at the same time.* Excluded by that condition are cases in which we perform an evil act now to prevent something bad in the future from happening. Third, we must sincerely intend the good effect and not the bad. In the hypothetical example, this would mean that the father would have to be sincerely intending to save his son and not simply committing suicide under the pretense of saving his son. The fourth condition speaks of a "proportionately grave reason" for permitting an evil effect to occur. In the hypothetical cases presented above, the father lost his life while saving the life of his son. This is a reasonable thing to do. If the father lost his life in order to save the family pet, it would most likely be judged an unreasonable thing to do.

The principle of double effect is applied in a limited number of cases dealing with abortion. An ectopic pregnancy results when the fertilized egg lodges in the fallopian tube. This is a non-viable pregnancy. If the tube bursts, the woman might bleed to death. When this condition is discovered a surgeon will remove the section of the fallopian tube in which the fertilized egg is lodged. If one believes that life begins at conception, then the surgeon has taken a life, but such actions are tolerated if the four conditions of the principle of double effect have been met. The action of the surgeon is morally good, or at least indifferent. The removal of a portion of the fallopian tube produces two effects at the same time. The surgeon intends to save the life of the woman and there is proportionate reason for performing the procedure. Since the four conditions have been met, this "indirect abortion" is tolerated. This principle is also applied in the case of a woman who has a cancerous uterus and must have that cancerous tissue removed to prevent her death. This principle may appear at first to be a wide loophole in the pro-life argument, but in practice the instances in which all four conditions are met are actually quite few.

Challenges to the Claim "Life Begins at Conception"

The first premise of the pro-life position states that life begins at conception. Pro-choice advocates have proposed other points in the nine-month gestation period as being the beginning point of personhood. The logic behind choosing a point past conception is that abortions prior to that point would be morally permissible because genuine human life does not yet exist. Of the many possible arguments that could be considered, we will examine four proposals that various thinkers have defended as being the beginning of personhood.

The latest possible point in the nine month continuum would be birth. While not frequently argued, this position regards the fetus as part of the woman's body over which she exercises complete control. Critics object that there is not a great deal of physiological difference between a newborn baby and a baby two weeks away from birth. This child could easily survive if born prematurely. The second proposal places personhood at the point at which the fetus can survive outside the mother's womb. This point in the development of a fetus is known as viability and is currently located at approximately the sixth month. Prior to that time, among other problems, the fetus lacks sufficient lung development to survive outside the womb. The U.S. Supreme Court placed great weight on viability when it rendered the *Roe v. Wade* decision. Many see this capability for physical independence as the point at which personhood arrives. Critics quickly point out that viability depends solely upon the currently available medical technology. We now have the technology to enable premature babies to survive who would have died if they were born thirty years ago. In the future we may have technology or medical advancements that would allow extremely premature children to live. Perhaps at some future date we will have artificial wombs in which fetuses could be brought to full term. A third proposal marks the beginning of personhood at the appearance of the brain wave in approximately the eighth week. Those who support this position argue that since the end of human life is defined as the absence of a brain wave, the beginning of human life should be dated at the first appearance of a brain wave. A fourth proposal would see personhood as beginning at roughly the second or third week after conception. At this stage in its development the fertilized egg reaches the critical point that determines whether or not the pregnancy will result in twins. Prior to this point it is unclear whether there is one child or two, so proponents maintain it would be premature to speak of personhood as properly existing during that period of time in the gestation process.[5] Fixing the beginning of personhood at two to three weeks after conception has the practical difficulty of the woman possibly not knowing she is pregnant, but it does allow the use of drugs that either prevent implantation of the fertilized egg or cause the woman's body to reject an egg that is already implanted.

The pro-life advocates would charge that the very project of determining a point after conception at which human life begins is mistaken. Viability, the appearance of a brain wave, or twinning occurs only in the case of a fertilized human egg. That sequence of events will not occur if the egg is not fertilized or with any other cell in the body. The facts indicate, according to the pro-life camp, that life begins at conception and that the process of gestation is a nine month unfolding of human personhood in greater and greater complexity. Brain waves do not simply appear; rather, the appearance of a brain wave is one step in the awe-inspiring process of fetal development that began at the moment of conception.

Some thinkers do not regard the biological development as the only factor (or even the most important factor) in determining the beginning of life. These thinkers do not deem a fertilized human egg the moral equivalent of a newborn baby. The fertilized egg, they insist, lacks some quality which distinguishes "a person" from other forms of life (e.g., self-awareness, creativity). Critics fear that such definitions of "personhood" often seem to exclude the retarded, senile, or comatose from being persons.

Challenges to the Claim: "The Direct Taking of Innocent Human Life Is Always Wrong"

The second premise of the pro-life position is that the direct taking of innocent human life is always wrong. As is the case with the first premise, this proposition has provoked a good deal of debate. We will examine four challenges to that claim.

The first argument revolves around the concept of "quality of life." Quality of life arguments offer some account of what constitutes a minimally acceptable standard of living. Should a person's quality of life fall below that level of existence, then abortion would not only be permissible, but in many cases it would be regarded as the better course of action. The quality of life argument in abortion takes one of two forms. The first focuses on the physical condition of the child, the second on the environment into which the child will be born. In the former, if parents were to discover through genetic testing that a child had an incurable, degenerative disease that would claim the child's life by age two or three, then some would argue that the parents could ethically choose to abort the fetus. In the second case, we are asked to consider the case of a child born into abject poverty. If starvation and lack of health care await the child, it would be morally acceptable, some argue, for an abortion to take place.

Pro-life advocates reject such "quality of life" arguments. First, they would insist that all life is sacred since all life is a gift from God. The dignity of the individual does not derive from its agreement with some socially determined set of criteria, but from the fact that all humans are created in the image of God. Second, pro-life supporters would fear the consequences of such thinking. If we begin to determine who lives and who dies, where does this end? This is known as a "slippery slope" argument. With the absolute prohibition against all direct abortions we stand on solid ground, but once "quality of life" considerations are introduced we step off the solid ground and step foot onto the "slippery slope." If we begin to allow abortions, for example, in cases of profound fetal deformity, what prevents us from justifying abortions in cases of moderate fetal deformity, and then mild fetal deformity? We move from the solid ground of permitting no abortions down the slippery slope until we hit bottom where we allow abortions for the most insignificant of reasons. We end up justifying the "elimination" of all types of people who prove "burdensome" to us. Finally, pro-life supporters insist that the answer to unwanted pregnancies or pregnancies that would result in any type of hardship is not abortion, but adoption.

The second pro-choice challenge concerns cases of rape and incest. Pro-choice advocates insist that a woman who is raped is under no moral obligation to continue that pregnancy. The most famous analogy in this regard was offered by Judith Jarvis Thomson twenty years ago.[6] Imagine a person wakes one morning to discover that a famous violinist with a severe kidney condition is now attached to that person's body. The person serves as the sole means of life support for the violinist. Thomson asks whether the person is morally obligated to stay attached to this person for nine months to sustain the violinist's life. The person, according to Thomson, is under no moral *obligation* to do so; if the person should choose to do so, certainly that person has that right, but there is not an obligation to do so. In the same way, a woman who has been victimized by a rapist is under no moral obligation to continue a pregnancy that will remind her of her painful assault.

The pro-life reply would be that abortion in cases of rape punishes the wrong party. The criminal who deserves punishment is the rapist and only the rapist. The woman is an innocent party, as is the fetus that is conceived through the act of rape. To punish either one would be highly immoral. Regarding the treatment of rape victims, Vincent J. Genovesi, S.J. writes,

> The official Roman Catholic teaching regarding the treatment of rape victims may be summarized this way: it is morally permissible, and even appropriate, to attempt to prevent conception from occurring in such instances; so long as there is a reasonable doubt that conception has occurred, properly indicated medical procedures may be initiated to forestall conception, but nothing may be done once that point in time has been reached when it may reasonably be expected that fertilization has already occurred, if indeed it is going to occur at all. The church adopts this position because in her eyes from the moment of conception a new person is present whose life we are fully bound to respect and protect.[7]

Genovesi quotes a textbook in medical ethics from 1955 which permits contraceptive treatment for rape victims up to ten hours after the act of rape.

The third situation proposed by pro-choice advocates would be cases in which the mother's life is endangered. There are two arguments used to justify abortion in these cases. The first is a variation of a self-defense argument. If the fetus threatens the life of the mother, then the fetus has become in some sense an unjust aggressor on the life of the mother. The abortion is then an act of self-preservation. The second argument is more utilitarian. Suppose the mother is a widow with three young children at home. If she continues the pregnancy she will leave her three children orphaned, so she therefore decides to have an abortion. Pro-life supporters would reject such argumentation, insisting that all life is precious and is not weighed against other concerns, no matter how well intentioned that may be.

The fourth situation proposed by pro-choice advocates would be cases of population control. Here again the argument is utilitarian. If a country (e.g., China) is densely populated, then consideration must be given to both present and future generations. If the food supply is not sufficient for unlimited population growth, then the government has the right, perhaps even the obligation, to curtail the rate of population growth. Governmental enforcement of abortion would therefore be justified. Pro-life supporters reject this argument, again invoking the principle that all human life is sacred and not to be bartered for some greater social good.

May a Catholic vote for a pro-choice candidate?

A related question to stem from the abortion debate concerns the role of Catholics holding public office and the obligations of Catholics casting votes for politicians. Is it ethical for a Catholic in public office to support pro-choice legislation? Is it ethical for a Catholic to vote for a pro-choice candidate? These questions raise a series of questions dealing with issues such as the separation of church and state, public and private morality, political practicality, etc. The flash point for this debate occurred in 1984 when Mario Cuomo, then governor of New York, delivered a lecture entitled "Religious Belief and Public Morality: A Catholic Governor's Perspective" at the University of Notre Dame.[8]

The issue arises from Mario Cuomo's affirmation of his personal belief that the church's position on abortion is morally correct. This is the crux of the dilemma. Is it possible to be in agreement with church teaching in one's personal life as a member of the Catholic Church, yet separate that belief from one's role as a politician in the public realm? Cuomo states, "As a Catholic I accept the church's teaching authority....As Catholics my wife and I were enjoined never to use abortion to destroy the life we created, and we never have. We thought church doctrine was clear on this, and—more than that—both of us felt it in full agreement with what our hearts and our consciences told us."[9] Cuomo, however, defends his position that Catholics who seek to enact legislation to prohibit abortions are wrong.

David Carlin contends that in his speech at Notre Dame, Cuomo offers two distinct arguments in support of his position. Carlin defines the first as a "religious pluralism" argument: "In a religiously diverse society like the United States we are free to practice our own religiously distinctive moral values, but we are not free to impose these on others."[10] Cuomo states, "The Catholic public official lives the political truth most Catholics through most of American history have accepted and insisted on: the truth that to assure our freedom we must allow others the same freedom, even if occasionally it produces conduct by them, which we would hold to be sinful."[11] Carlin labels the second argument the "impracticality of enforcement" argument: even if anti-abortion legislation could be enacted, we could not make it work. Cuomo argues, "I believe that legal interdicting of abortion by either the federal government or the individual states is not a plausible possibility and even if it could be obtained, it wouldn't work. Given present attitudes, it would be Prohibition revisited, legislating what couldn't be enforced and in the process creating a disrespect for law in general."[12]

There has been much debate about the arguments Cuomo put forth in his Notre Dame address. Some have found his plea for "political realism" both pragmatic and responsible. Others remain unconvinced. In opposition to the "religious pluralism" argument, critics charge that abortion is not simply a "religious" issue, i.e., an atheist could oppose abortion on moral grounds. If Cuomo had forbidden the serving of meat in New York restaurants on the Fridays of Lent, then one could argue that he was imposing a religious morality, but abortion does not fall into the same category. Even if the opposition to abortion is religiously rooted, the idea can be advocated on non-religious grounds. For example, if someone became committed to the civil rights movement of the 1960s because of the preaching of ministers in southern congregations, this would not relegate such concerns to being purely "religious concerns" that could not be "imposed" on the general populace. Others have criticized the impracticality argument on the basis that such an argument justifies a lack of moral courage on the part of the politician and allows the politician to avoid politically unpopular positions. Political leadership entails taking unpopular positions when necessary.

Other Unresolved Questions

In addition to the controversial questions presently swirling around the abortion debate which we have discussed, there are other relevant questions that have been raised. Public debate continues on the federal funding of abortion, mandatory waiting periods, and parental permission laws. We conclude with one area that has received a great deal of attention, but still awaits resolution.

This area of controversy that strikes at the heart of the debate involves the constitutional question of rights. In the American political tradition we stand in the interesting position of insisting that rights be upheld and protected, yet we recognize that few rights are absolute. For example, we are guaranteed the right to free speech. Despite this, the law does not recognize slander as a legitimate expression of that right and such behavior is legally prohibited. Discussion about rights involves wise decisions about which behavior is protected by that constitutionally guaranteed right and which behavior is not protected.

In order to clarify this discussion of rights, consider the two following statements.

(1) "I am personally opposed to eating red meat, but will allow others to do so."

(2) "I am personally opposed to keeping slaves, but will allow others to do so."

The first statement will strike most readers as a reasonable position. A person may for health reasons or ethical reasons choose not to eat red meat, even wish that everyone would do the same, but still realize that legal interdiction of eating meat would be unjustified. By contrast, the second statement is ludicrous. Opposition to slavery is not simply a statement of personal preference, it is a statement about the dignity and equality of all persons. Returning to the abortion debate, consider the following statement in light of the two early ones: "I am personally opposed to abortion, but others should be able to have one if they so desire." The question is, "Does this proposition more closely resemble the statement regarding the eating of red meat or the keeping of slaves?"

Pro-choice advocates argue for the former, pro-life advocates argue for the latter. If it more closely resembles the former, then pro-life activists are imposing their morality on others. If it is the latter, then pro-choice activists are denying fundamental rights to the unborn.

The furor over abortion shows no signs of abating in the near future. Both sides feel they are upholding a value of supreme importance. For Christians, questions of constitutionality and rights are important, but for them the debate will never be solely about these issues. In whichever camp they stand, Christians must ground their position in their understanding of discipleship. Quarrels arose among disciples in Jesus' day and throughout the past two thousand years. The cost of this particular dispute, however, may prove to be very high indeed.

Discussion Questions

1. What is your position on abortion?
2. What is the best argument in opposition to your position? How would you respond to that argument?
3. May Catholics vote for a pro-choice candidate?
4. Should parental permission be required for minors seeking abortions?
5. Should federal funds be used for abortions?

Suggested Readings

The official church position on abortion can be found in the *Declaration on Abortion* (Washington, D.C.: United States Catholic Conference, 1974), issued by the Congregation for the Doctrine of the Faith. This also appears in Origins 4 (25) December 12, 1974.

Parish study groups may find *The Case Against Abortion: A Logical Argument for Life* by Lori Van Winden (Ligouri: Ligouri Publications, 1988) a useful text.

Students may find two anthologies helpful in identifying the arguments in the debate: *Abortion and Catholicism: The American Debate*, edited by Patricia Beattie Jung and Thomas Shannon (New York: Crossroad, 1988) and *Abortion: The Moral Issues*, edited by Edward Batchelor, Jr. (New York: Pilgrim Press, 1982). For an anthology devoted to the issue of "quality of life," see *Quality of Life: The New Medical Dilemma*, edited by James J. Walter and Thomas A. Shannon (Mahwah: Paulist Press, 1990).

See also Daniel Callahan's "An Ethical Challenge to Prochoice Advocates" in *Commonweal*, November 23, 1990. Callahan favors keeping abortion legal, but raises a number of concerns about current pro-choice thought.

Sexual Ethics

Discuss the following cases. Do they meet with your ethical approval? Why? Why not?

1. A college couple have been dating for two years and decide to live together. They share all expenses equally and use birth control. They have decided that in the event that the birth control fails and the woman should become pregnant, they will marry.

2. A lesbian couple has been involved in a monogamous relationship for almost ten years. Each woman's family is aware of their relationship and relates to them as if they were a married heterosexual couple.

3. A bill comes before a local town council that would grant legal status to homosexual marriages. A local representative votes in opposition to the proposal.

4. A twenty-five year old divinity student is soon to be ordained for ministry in a Protestant denomination that does not ordain "avowed, practicing homosexuals." A medium-sized congregation has offered him a job as pastor and he has accepted the position. He has worked at this church during the past two summers and the congregation has great praise for his work both in the

church and in the community. Feeling he would be "living a lie" by not publicly acknowledging his sexual orientation, he informs both the church and the governing body of his denomination that he is a homosexual. Although not presently involved in a relationship, he does not preclude the possibility at some point in his life. The church indicates that they would still like to have him as their pastor, but the governing body refuses to ordain him.

5. A married heterosexual couple feel that after twenty years of marriage their sex life has become lifeless, so they mutually agree that they should "swing" with other partners.

6. A young married couple is involved in a serious car accident during the first year of their marriage. The woman is left permanently comatose. After ten years of caring for his wife, the husband begins to date another woman. The man vows to provide financial support for his wife until her death, but feels "I should get on with my life," so he divorces his wife and marries the second woman.

7. In an effort to reduce the rate of sexually transmitted disease and pregnancy in the local public high school, the school board begins a condom distribution program in the school. Students may receive, without charge, a condom from either the school nurse or health teacher. Parental permission is not required.

What constitutes appropriate and inappropriate sexual behavior on the part of Christians? This discussion stirs volatile debate within the church and the wider society. Our examination of this issue begins by clarifying the differences between two different approaches in moral reasoning. Without an awareness of these differences, parties in this conversation often speak *at* each other rather than *with* each other. We move then to a review of the debate with the Catholic community regarding heterosexual activity outside of marriage and conclude by turning our attention to the question of homosexuality.

Moral Reasoning

Before discussing specific cases, we need to differentiate between two different types of moral reasoning commonly employed in the discussion of sexual ethics. We discussed in chapter one the difference between a consequentialist and non-consequentialist approach to morality. A consequentialist looks at the results in order to arrive at a decision regarding the morality or immorality of a particular action. A non-consequentialist does not determine the morality of an act by the consequences that follow from it, but instead looks at the very act itself to determine if it is morally acceptable or not. Applying that discussion to this particular issue, we can detect significant differences between how consequentialist and non-consequentialist thinkers go about making a moral argument. Suppose a high school couple consider having sex. The young woman confides in her close friend her interest in having sex with her boyfriend. Her friend then asks, "What if you get pregnant?" That very practical concern expresses a form of consequentialist reasoning. The friend is asking the young woman to consider the consequences of her actions. Suppose instead her friend says, "But you don't even love him." That response would represent a different approach. Here the friend does not appeal to consequences; rather, she evaluates the proposal on the basis of her understanding of what sex entails. Since she believes sex should be an expression of love, she disapproves of friend's intention to engage in sex with a young man whom she believes her friend does not love.

It is important to remember that consequentialist and non-consequentialist moral reasoning are ways of making a moral argument; they do not necessarily represent specific conclusions. A consequentialist looks at the results: if the results are favorable, then the action is morally justifiable. Some couples looking at the possible results may find them highly desirable; other couples looking at the very same results may find them frightful. The non-consequentialist approach also does not immediately translate into one specific conclusion. The non-consequentialist begins with an understanding of what sex is. Some may regard sex as a pleasurable experience between two consenting adults. Others may regard sex as an expression of the divinely willed covenant between husband and wife. When considering the morality of a sexually active couple who live together without being married, those who view sex as a pleasurable experience between two consenting adults would have no problem with that arrangement; those who regard sex as an expression of the divinely willed covenant of husband and wife would find that arrangement immoral.

By situating this discussion in terms of the Christian way of life, we need to understand that this casts the arguments in a certain light. First, the Christian tradition believes the human person to be both body and soul, or flesh and spirit. Paul speaks of the body as "the temple of the Holy Spirit" (1 Cor 6:19). It follows therefore that sexual activity is not simply a physical, biological experience. Second, sex will always be a big deal for Christians because they regard sex as part of the divine plan by which human love is expressed and human life is generated. Christians therefore oppose those attitudes which trivialize or cheapen the inherent dignity of sex. Third, sexual behavior, as is the case with all morally significant behavior, is a matter of choice. The Catholic tradition has preserved a tradition of witness by men and women in religious communities who have chosen the single life as their way of responding to the call of the gospel. They testify by their lives to the belief that a man or woman can live a personally fulfilling and religiously satisfying life without marriage and family.

Debates Within the Roman Catholic Community

The official Roman Catholic position regarding sexual ethics can be found in the 1975 *Declaration on Certain Questions Concerning Sexual Ethics.* The Declaration asserts that the teaching concerning sexual ethics is based in the divine law which we know through reason. "These fundamental principles, which can be grasped by reason, are contained in the 'divine law'—eternal, objective and universal—whereby God orders, directs and governs the entire universe and all the ways of the human community, by a plan conceived in wisdom and love. Man has been made by God to participate in this law.... This divine law is accessible to our minds."[1] It is important to recall the natural law approach discussed earlier. According to this, human reason serves as a reliable guide in ethical matters. That reasoning process, of course, requires the additional guidance of divine revelation, though these two sources of ethical wisdom do not conflict since both are from God. Relying upon human reason, we can ask, "What is the purpose of sexual activity?" The Declaration insists that Vatican II "took particular care to expound the principles and criteria which concern human sexuality in marriage, and which are based upon the finality of the specific function of sexuality."[2] The finality of the sexual act is twofold (and this repeats the teaching of the bishops at Vatican II): mutual self-giving and procreation. The Declaration insists that "it is respect for its finality [of the sexual act] that ensures the moral goodness of this act."[3] How is that moral goodness of sexual relations preserved? Drawing upon revelation we learn that God ordained that such goals be realized in marriage. "Through marriage, in fact, the love of married people is taken up into that love which Christ irrevocably has for the Church, while dissolute sexual union defiles the temple of the Holy Spirit which the Christian has become. Sexual union therefore is only legitimate if a definitive community of life has been established between the man and the woman."[4] On this basis, the Declaration condemns premarital, extramarital, and homosexual activity.

Two years after the Vatican Declaration there appeared a study commission by the Catholic Theological Society of America. Entitled *Human Sexuality* this study challenged not only the conclusions of the Declaration, but the very way in which the Declaration approached the subject of sexual ethics. The study worried that the traditional Catholic evaluation of sexual behavior was concerned solely with the gender and marital status of the person involved. In other words, the traditional position gave inadequate attention to the relationship shared by the two persons. Instead of focusing on the physical aspect of the sexual relationship, ethicists should look first to the emotional, spiritual, and affective dimensions of the relationship. Sex needs to be seen in the larger context of human sexuality. "Sexuality is not just an isolated biological or physical phenomenon accidental to human beings but an integral part of their personal self-expression and their mission of self-communication to others."[5] The authors insist that sexual behavior should be judged according to how well it fosters "integration." They write, "Wholesome sexual activity is that which fosters a creative growth toward integration. Destructive sexuality results in personal frustration and interpersonal alienation."[6] The authors propose the following values as characteristics of sexual behavior which promotes integration:

a. self-liberating: the sexual activity should foster "personal growth towards maturity"
b. other-enriching: the sexual activity should give "expression to a generous interest and concern for the well-being of the other"
c. honest: the sexual expression should express "openly and candidly and as truthfully as possible the depth of the relationship"
d. faithful: the sexual activity should facilitate "the development of stable relationships"
e. socially responsible: sexual activity should reflect "the relationship and responsibility of the individuals to the larger community (family, nation, world)"
f. life-serving: sexual activity should give expression to this life-serving quality in creative ways (e.g., procreation or dedicated service to people)
g. joyous: sexual activity should "give witness to exuberant appreciation of the gift of life and (the) mystery of love"[7]

The morality of sexual expression therefore depends not upon marriage, but upon the degree to which the relationship manifests these values.

Homosexuality

This debate carries over into the discussion of homosexuality. The 1986 *Letter to the Bishops of the Catholic Church on the Pastoral Care of Homosexual Persons* repeats the traditional teaching. "It is only in the marital relationship that the use of the sexual faculty can be morally good. A person engaging in homosexual behavior therefore acts immorally."[8] The Congregation for the Doctrine of the Faith based this condemnation of homosexual activity on two sources: natural law and scripture. In terms of the former, since natural sexual inclination is directed toward members of the opposite sex, homosexual orientation represents, in the words of the letter, "a disordered sexual inclination."[9] In terms of the latter, the letter refers to many of the frequently cited scriptural verses which denounce homosexual activity. The bishops mention the story of Sodom and Gomorrah which will be discussed in greater detail later (Gn 19:1–11), the passages in the "holiness codes" of Leviticus (Lev 18:22; 20:13), and three passages from the New Testament (1 Cor 6:9; Rom 1:18–32; 1 Tim 1:10).

The debate regarding the morality of homosexuality includes an important distinction. We need to differentiate between "homosexual orientation" and "homosexual activity." Homosexual orientation refers to the attraction a person experiences toward members of the same sex. This is distinguished from the actual physical engagement in sexual acts with members of the same sex that constitutes homosexual activity. With that distinction, we will review four different responses to the question, "What should be the proper response of the Christian community toward homosexuality?"

The first school of thought condemns both homosexual activity and orientation. Basing their position on natural law and scriptural arguments, advocates of this position condemn homosexual activity, but, more than that, they also condemn the sexual inclination of the homosexual. The condemnation of sexual inclination remains this position's most problematic feature. If sexual orientation is not freely chosen, then it seems unreasonable to condemn someone on that basis alone.

The second school of thought also regards homosexual activity as immoral for the reasons already cited. However, in this school of thought, sexual inclination is not itself grounds for moral condemnation. The inclination may be "disordered," but the person who experiences such an inclination is not excluded from the Christian community. The scientific community continues to offer hypotheses for the origin of homosexual and heterosexual orientation, but to date the origins of those drives are largely unknown. The moral condemnation of homosexual activity continues, but the celibate homosexual is welcomed into the church. The Roman Catholic Church endorses this position regarding homosexuality.

The third school of thought gives great consideration to the issue of homosexual orientation. The homosexual orientation experienced by one person may arise suddenly after years of heterosexual orientation; for another person that type of sexual inclination may have been with him or her since that person's awakening of sexual desire. This school of thought concentrates on the second type of orientation. For those who have an "irreversible" homosexual orientation and have integrated their sexuality into the personality in a psychologically positive way, the physical expression of that sexual inclination may be acceptable. Fr. Charles Curran writes, "(F)or an irreversible or constitutional homosexual, homosexual acts in the context of a loving relationship striving for permanency can be and are morally good."[10] There is an important point to be added here. Proponents insist that this conclusion should be regarded as a "compromise position." Heterosexual marriage, in other words, remains the ideal, but other forms of sexual expression could be allowed.

The fourth school of thought evaluates all sexual activity on the basis of the quality of the relationship. If the relationship is supportive, nurturing, compassionate, etc., then the activity is moral, regardless of the sexual orientation or the gender of the two persons involved in the relationship. This school of thought places the greatest weight on the type of relationship in which sexual expression takes place, and places the least weight on the gender or marital status of the persons involved.

This fourth position raises a number of issues regarding marriage and family. Is a union of two loving, mutually supportive homosexuals the moral equivalent of the union between two loving, mutually supportive heterosexuals? Should a gay couple have as much right as a heterosexual couple to adopt children? In some respects these questions revolve around how one understands "family." What constitutes a "family"? The traditional answer is, of course, the nuclear family consisting of a husband and a wife with children. Does the nuclear family represent the ideal family unit against which all other family arrangements are to be measured, or does the nuclear family represent one of many equally valid instances of family? If the nuclear family remains the ideal, then homosexual marriage, if allowed at all, would be tolerated more than celebrated. Adoption would be either discouraged or disallowed. If a wide range of domestic arrangements are put on a par with the nuclear family, then a variety of lifestyles and contexts for child-rearing would be embraced by the Christian community.

Concluding Thoughts

These four perspectives represent a sampling of conclusions reached by Christian communities grappling with the issue of homosexuality. These four perspectives serve as the basis by which related controversial issues are debated. For example, should the church ordain a practicing homosexual to ministry in a Christian church? While the Catholic Church would not ordain a practicing homosexual, various Protestant denominations have done so. Those in the first two schools of thought would oppose such ordinations. Those in the third school of thought might allow such ordinations under certain conditions. Those in the fourth school of thought would have no problem with the practice.

The issues involved in this debate are numerous: the authority and proper interpretation of scripture, the status of natural law claims, and the place of the family in the Christian way of life. In terms of the role of scripture in this debate, we encounter a double problem. First, there is the discussion of the weight one should give the literal words of scripture when arriving at a moral decision. Even if one should give great weight to scripture, there remains the question of how to settle disputes in biblical interpretation. For example, interpreters differ on their interpretation of the story of the destruction of Sodom and Gomorrah (Gn 18–19). In this story angels visit the city of Sodom because they have heard of the city's wickedness. Appearing as ordinary men, these angels arrive in Sodom and are greeted by Abraham's nephew, Lot, who offers them lodging in his house for the night and feeds them. That night, the men of Sodom arrive at Lot's house and demand that these visitors be brought out to them so that they may sexually abuse them. Eventually the men press against the door. The angels throw them back with a beam of light and tell Lot to gather his family and head for the hills. The cities of Sodom and Gomorrah are then destroyed by fire and brimstone. Interpreters generally agree that this story expresses the common theme of divine retribution against human sinfulness. They debate, however, the sin being punished. Interpreters have traditionally read this story as a condemnation of the homosexual activity of the townsmen. Other commentators argue that the sin of Sodom and Gomorrah is the inhospitable behavior of the townsmen toward the stranger, which in this particular case took a sexual form. Writing in the *New York Times*, Peter Gomes offers the following interpretation of the story: "...recall that the story is not about sexual perversion and homosexual practice. It is about inhospitality, according to Luke 10:10–13 and failure to care for the poor, according to

Ezekiel 16:49–50: 'Behold, this was the iniquity of thy sister Sodom, pride, fullness of bread, and abundance of idleness was in her and in her daughters, neither did she strengthen the hand of the poor and needy.' To suggest that Sodom and Gomorrah is about homosexual sex is an analysis of about as much worth as suggesting that the story of Jonah and the whale is a treatise on fishing."[11]

The questions of sexual intimacy continue to generate a great deal of controversy. The issues here are numerous. How important is the Bible? How should the biblical stories be interpreted? Does a natural law exist? Is compromise a good thing or a bad thing for the church? In the midst of these debates exist the Christian couple who must make decisions about their sexual behavior. This most intimate of situations has given rise to one of the church's most vocal public debates.

Discussion Questions

1. Is it ever ethically permissible for Christians to engage in heterosexual relations outside of marriage?
2. Which perspective should the church take toward homosexuality?
3. How important is the Bible in your moral reasoning about sexual matters?
4. Would it bother you if your child, roommate, or friend disclosed that he or she was a homosexual?

Suggested Readings

The official church teaching on sexual ethics can be found in the *Declaration on Certain Questions Concerning Sexual Ethics* (Washington, D.C.: United States Catholic Conference, 1975) and the *Letter to the Bishops of the Catholic Church on the Pastoral Care of Homosexual Persons* (Washington, D.C.: United States Catholic Conference,

1986). See also *Human Sexuality: A Catholic Perspective for Education and Lifelong Learning* (Washington, D.C.: United States Catholic Conference, 1991).

For a defense of the church's position see *Catholic Sexual Ethics: A Summary, Explanation,* and *Defense* by Ronald Lawler, O.F.M, Cap., Joseph M. Boyle, Jr., and William E. May (Huntington: Our Sunday Visitor, 1985). For a summary of differing approaches to the issue, see *What Are They Saying About Sexual Morality?* by James P. Hanigan (New York: Paulist, 1982), chapters four and five. See also *Between the Sexes: Foundations for a Christian Ethics of Sexuality* by Lisa Sowle Cahill (Philadelphia: Fortress, 1985).

For an overview of the positions in the debate over homosexuality, see *Homosexuality and Ethics* (New York: Pilgrim Press, 1980), edited by Edward Batchelor. For a sympathetic commentary on the *Letter to the Bishops of the Catholic Church on the Pastoral Care of Homosexual Persons* , see John R. Quinn, "Toward an Understanding of the Letter 'On the Pastoral Care of Homosexual Persons,' " in *The Vatican and Homosexuality*, edited by Jeannine Gramick and Pat Furey (New York: Crossroad, 1988). For a helpful survey of the dissenting theological positions, see chapter five of *The Homosexual Person: New Thinking in Pastoral Care* by John F. Harvey, O.S.F.S. (San Francisco: Ignatius Press, 1987).

Social Justice

Discuss the following cases. What is the just thing to do in each?

1. Citing increased competition from overseas firms with much lower overhead costs, the management of a textile mill seeks concessions from the union. The union balks and the corporation closes the factory and moves to another state where labor costs are lower.

2. A prosperous nation is separated by a small body of water from the poorest nation in the hemisphere. The government of the prosperous nation decides that it will no longer accept into the country any citizen of the poorer nation who has tested positive for AIDS.

3. An unmarried pregnant woman lives in poverty in a poor nation with high unemployment. Only a narrow river separates this nation from a much wealthier country. Knowing that any child born in the wealthier nation will have automatic citizenship and access to its educational and health care systems, the woman crosses the river illegally, stays with friends, and gives birth to a baby boy two weeks later.

4. A politician introduces a bill into the state legislature that

would limit the amount of welfare assistance a single mother may receive. Specifically, the bill mandates that a single mother who is on welfare may not receive additional funds for the children born to her while she is receiving assistance from the state. Advocates argue this bill will reduce the number of children on welfare. Critics charge that such a bill will end up hurting the children born into poverty.

5. A small farmer has been raising wheat for years. Shortly after purchasing a sizable tract of land, the government implements certain trade policies that cause a glut of wheat on the world market. The price of wheat falls considerably. Unable to make payments on the loan taken to purchase the new tract of land, the farmer is about to lose his farm. A powerful senator from that state is able to include in an unrelated bill governmental subsidies for grain. The bill passes; the farmer receives the subsidies and is able to make payments on the loan.

6. A presidential candidate proposes that we convert our tax system from a progressive system in which those with higher incomes pay a larger percentage of their income in taxes to a flat tax system in which all citizens pay the same percentage of their income in taxes.

7. An employee files a lawsuit against a corporation doing work for the government, claiming the corporation has been engaging in discrimination in its hiring and promotion decisions. The employee wins the suit. The court also orders the corporation to set hiring goals and establish timetables by which those goals will be met.

Although Jesus had much to say about love of neighbor and the dangers of wealth, he did not leave us with a blueprint for how society should be organized. It falls to humans to fashion political and economic structures that best promote the cause of social justice. In the United States debates over social policy take place in the halls of congress, in local town councils, and at dinner tables across the country. Given the separation of church and state, the church does not enjoy any privileged standing in this debate, but neither is it excluded from participating in it. Believing that the Catholic tradition offers many valuable insights into the nature of justice, the Catholic bishops in the United States felt compelled to comment on the nation's economic system. This they did in their pastoral letter *Economic Justice for All* in 1986. We begin by placing this letter in the broader tradition of political and economic theory.

A Christian Political or Economic Theory?

Though the Bible certainly has much to say about how people should relate to each other, it does not present a unified theory of political and economic justice. Consequently, Christians have generally drawn on the work of thinkers in the fields of philosophy or economics when constructing a systematic, full-blown "Christian political philosophy" or "theory of Christian economics." Some theories were readily taken over by Christian thinkers to serve as the vehicle for their thought, while others were almost unanimously rejected. For example, theories that elevate the pursuit of self-interest to the level of the supreme good have been deemed by the vast majority of Christian thinkers to be incompatible with the gospel message. By contrast, Thomas Aquinas, the great medieval Christian philosopher and theologian, drew extensively from the work of the great Greek philosopher Aristotle. Though criticized for relying on the work of a "pagan philosopher," Aquinas developed Aristotle's idea that things in this world exist for a certain purpose or tend toward a certain natural goal. Just as acorns naturally move in their development toward becoming oak trees, humans naturally seek certain goals (e.g., life in a peaceful, orderly society). Aquinas saw in this way of thinking an affirmation of the Christian worldview which sees all things in this world participating in a grand design ordained by God. All things come from God, move with God, and return to God. The justice of political and economic arrangements was measured by the extent to which they safeguarded these natural goals. This perspective continues to inform many of the church's statements on social justice.

Rival Starting Points in Political and Economic Theory

When Christians have turned to the systematic theories of secular philosophers to serve as their vehicles for presenting a Christian theory of politics or economics, their choices have been varied. Within this variety, however, two prominent schools of thought vie for their allegiance. Both cite biblical passages in support of their claims, though each starting point historically leads to radically different conclusions about what constitutes a just political or economic system. The first school of thought seeks to safeguard at all turns the autonomy of the individual. Since priority is given to the individual, we will label this first group of thinkers "individualists." The second school of thought believes that the wider community has legitimate claims which must be weighed against individual autonomy. Since the second group places great weight on the life of the community as a whole, we will label them "communitarians." As James Sterba notes, "Like Aristotle, communitarians endorse a fundamental contrast between humans beings as they are and human beings as they could be if they realized their essential nature. Ethics is then viewed as a science that enables human beings to understand how they can make the transition from the former state to the latter."[1]

To illustrate the differences between the two approaches, let us consider a hypothetical example. Suppose a small corporation has an informal policy that allows employees to leave work early should a school nurse call with news that their child is sick. During a particularly harsh flu season many employees leave work to pick up their children from school. Employees who do not have children begin to complain that this policy is not fair since the departure of these parents generates a greater work load for them. Should this informal policy be reversed? Of course, one would need to know, among other things, what additional burden this policy places on the other employees, but let us assume that the burden is not unreasonable and that the parents do not abuse this policy. One school of thought would insist that such a policy infringes on the rights of the individual who is not a parent since this results in a greater work load for that person. Another school of thought would see the care of children as a common concern for all members of society, not only of individual parents. Since the policy benefits children whose welfare are our common concern, such a policy is just.[2]

Both approaches accord the individual great value, but they differ in a number of important ways. We will discuss four of the most important differences. First, these two schools of thought differ in their understanding of society. For the individualists, society is a collection of individuals who are seeking goals they find personally satisfying. For the communitarians, society is a collective whole seeking certain common goals. The former group wishes to maximize individual initiative, creativity, and self-expression. The latter group values social cooperation and human solidarity. Second, these two groups differ over the role government should play in the life of the society. Since the interests of individuals may conflict, the individualists see a role for government in establishing and maintaining a suitable level of protection against coercion or violence, but for them the government that governs least governs best. For the communitarians, humans are "political" by nature in the sense that they flourish in community (i.e., "the polis"). Government plays an integral role in the life of the community and leaders are entrusted with enacting laws that will benefit the common good. The third difference concerns taxation and government spending. The individualists insist that personal wealth (assuming it was fairly acquired in freely chosen economic exchanges between competent parties) rightly belongs to that person. That person should be under no obligation to pay a greater percentage of income in taxes nor is the government justified in taking money from that person in order to fund programs that benefit "special interest" groups. Instead of using government subsidies to bail out a troubled industry, for example, the forces at work in a free market should be allowed to resolve the problem. The communitarians see the common good calling upon members of society with greater wealth to assume a greater tax burden in terms of percentage of income earned. A flat tax of twenty-five percent, for example, would result in a significantly greater burden on poorer families than it would on wealthier families. The common good also requires all citizens to finance programs that serve the needs of the wider community, and which the taxpayers themselves may never use. All citizens, for example, have an obligation to fund the public school system, even if they have no children who will benefit from that school system. Finally, the fourth difference is directly related to the pastoral letter on the economy. If the bishops are to speak out against perceived injustices in the American economic system, what type of analysis and proposals should they offer? For the individualists, the appropriate strategy would be to address themselves to the consciences of individual Catholics and encourage them to seek solutions which bring about greater social justice. The communitarians would encourage the bishops to actively engage in social analysis and address structural problems in the economic system of the community (e.g., trade policies, poverty programs).

Economic Justice for All

We now turn our attention to the bishops' letter on the economy to see where they stand in the debates discussed above. When outlining the principal themes of their letter, the bishops identify the following as their first principle: *"Every economic decision and institution must be judged in light of whether it protects or undermines the dignity of the individual human person.* The pastoral letter begins with the human person."[3] This first principal theme does not directly locate the document in either the individualist or the communitarian school of thought. The second theme, however, clarifies the situation. *"Human dignity can be realized and protected only in community.* In our teaching, the human person is not only sacred but social....The obligation to 'love our neighbor' has an individual dimension, but it also requires a broader social commitment to the common good."[4] The attention given to the "common good" is most telling. The bishops declare, "Vatican II described the common good as the 'sum total of those conditions of social life which allow social groups and their individual members relatively thorough and ready access to their own fulfillment.' These conditions include the rights to fulfillment of material needs, a guarantee of fundamental freedoms, and the protection of relationships that are essential to participation in the life of society."[5] The concept of the common good also requires that we be especially diligent in protecting the poor and the vulnerable in our society. So while the bishops do spend a good deal of time discussing the importance of human rights and the need to protect the rights of the individual, they also speak of human solidarity and the "communitarian vocation" of human beings.[6]

This tension between protecting the rights of the individual and promoting the common good surfaces as well in the bishops' view toward the role of government. The bishops insist that government should not do what individuals can do on their own. In other words, governmental interference should be kept to a minimum. This respects the autonomy of the individual. On the other hand, the state has a moral obligation to protect the common good. The state does have a duty to insure proper education, housing, and health care for its citizens. This idea is known as the principle of subsidiarity. The bishops insist that this principle "provides space for freedom, initiative, and creativity on the part of many social agents. At the same time, it insists that all these agents should work in ways that help build up the social body."[7]

Preferential Treatment

We have considered the rival political and economic theories and the different conclusions one draws when giving priority to either the individual or the community. These considerations we have discussed so far are fairly abstract. It might be helpful, then, to apply these reflections to a specific question of social justice in order to illustrate how these abstractions directly impact one's thinking. The practice of preferential treatment or affirmative action remains one of the most controversial. Such programs identify certain groups who have been subject to discrimination in the past and give those groups special consideration in college admissions, hiring, or promotion in the workplace. Is such a system just? The American bishops believe so. "Where the effects of past discrimination persist, society has the obligation to take positive steps to overcome the legacy of injustice. Judiciously administered affirmative action programs in education and employment can be important expressions of the drive for solidarity and participation that is at the heart of true justice. Social harm calls for social relief."[8]

Those who argue for preferential treatment programs typically invoke two types of arguments. The first concerns justice. Justice, they insist, requires equal opportunity for advancement in society. The second argument follows closely upon the first. This "social realism" argument asks, "Do we live in a society in which all people have equal opportunity for advancement?" If we realistically evaluate our society, proponents charge, we will see that this is simply not the case. In their 1979 letter on racism *Brothers and Sisters to Us*, the American bishops wrote, "Today in our country men, women, and children are being denied opportunities for full participation and advancement in our society because of their race. The educational, legal, and financial systems, along with other structures and sectors of our society, impede people's progress and narrow their access because they are black, Hispanic, Native American or Asian."[9] In addition to discrimination on the basis of race, gender or creed, there exist other less obvious ways in which society does not provide equal opportunity. For example, public schools are commonly funded by the local property taxes. In those states in which such a funding policy exists, a student who by accident of birth was born in a wealthier community with higher property values will enroll in a better funded public school system than a student who by accident of birth was born in a community with lower property values. The school the first student attends may have computers and a music program that the second school simply can not afford. Proponents conclude, therefore, that we need to recognize these inequities and implement programs that will help balance the scales of justice so our society can approach more closely the ideal of equal opportunity for all.

Those who oppose preferential treatment programs advance two arguments of their own. First, they charge that such programs amount to reverse discrimination. One cannot condemn past discrimination on the basis of race, color, creed, or gender and then institute programs that now continue the practice. If discrimination was wrong then, it is wrong now. It's the "two wrongs don't make a right" argument. Furthermore, this policy punishes those who played no direct role in past discrimination. The second type of argument I will label "negative signals." This actually covers a host of arguments, but the general thrust of each of them is that such policies create undesirable situations in the workplace. For example, suppose in a particular plant employees regard the promotion to the position of plant supervisor as a reward for many years of exceptional work. Suppose further that this coveted promotion occurs about once every five years. If a fifty year old white man working on the floor of a plant learns that the company's new affirmative action policy dictates that the next three promotions must be given to minorities or women, he knows that his chances for promotion to the position of plant supervisor before his retirement at the age of sixty five are zero. Not only might his productivity decline, his pride in his work may also diminish. In addition to that, those promoted to the position of plant supervisor will not be accorded the respect enjoyed by previous supervisors since in the eyes of many employees their promotions were not based on merit.

Job promotion provides an interesting illustration of how difficult it is to achieve justice in the workplace. On what basis should promotions be given in the workplace? The first, and perhaps most obvious standard is performance. In sales positions, for example, promotions, perks, or increased commissions depend on the yearly total of sales for the company. Most regard this system as fair. The problem arises when one moves outside a field where results are easily quantified into areas such as teaching, nursing, or any number of other occupations where results are not so easily measured. The use of standardized tests provides a second way to determine promotions. This provides objectivity in scoring and judges the candidates' knowledge of a body of information generally regarded as essential for the job. The problem, of course, is that some people simply do not test well. They freeze up; their minds go blank. Many competent people simply do not score well on standardized tests. The third basis, seniority, acknowledges the person's years of experience and rewards loyalty to the firm. A trained car mechanic, for example, has years of experience of diagnosing car troubles which a younger mechanic simply does not have. This experience should help the mechanic diagnose a problem more quickly and repair it more efficiently. The problem, of course, is that experience does not equal expertise. Years alone do not necessarily establish competence. The fourth method, peer observation and evaluation, seems reasonable in that someone in the field should be best able to critique the work of someone engaged in that line of work. Especially in those fields where results are not easily quantified, it seems appropriate to have a knowledgeable supervisor evaluate that person's performance. Unfortunately the evaluator's subjectivity often colors the evaluation. In some cases, the evaluation reflects a personality conflict with the person being observed rather than being an objective assessment of that person's work.

College admissions present their own unique challenges in terms of justice. What is a just system for determining who should be admitted to a college or university? Questions abound. Should college admission be based solely on an applicant's academic record? Should extra-curricular activities be factored into the decision? Should athletes, children of alumni, veterans, state residents or children of benefactors be given preferential treatment in terms of college admissions? Each of these raises its own set of questions, but they all revolve around the concept of justice.

One final area brings many of the concerns we have discussed into focus. Some insist that a quota system is needed in college admissions or job hiring to insure a just representation of the general population in the halls of colleges and corporations across the country. In its most straightforward version, a quota system selects for admission or hiring a group of individuals whose ethnic, sexual, or racial composition reflects that of the wider society. A contract for construction of a federal office building, for example, may stipulate that the construction company's work force mirror the ethnic make-up of the surrounding populace. Such programs raise questions about the role of government, but they also bring into sharp contrast two different understandings of justice. The first sees justice as "equal opportunity." This school of thought rejects quotas since justice requires only that each person have an equal opportunity to apply for the job and be fairly evaluated on the basis of his or her performance. The second school of thought looks to results as the measure of whether justice has been served. Employers can too easily escape the demands of justice by conveniently claiming that everyone had "equal opportunity." Talk is cheap, they insist; the proof of a commitment to justice is seen in the results of the hiring process.

While Christians may share a common commitment to justice, they often disagree sharply over the means by which this justice is to be achieved. Despite the disruption this causes in the Christian community, these debates express the abiding concern Christians have for their neighbor. For while not the primary focus of the gospel message, political and economic policies do directly impact the living conditions of all human beings. Religious and economic concerns do therefore overlap. Christians in America will continue to voice concerns over economic policies that seem to embody values and priorities they find misguided. This pursuit of justice is but one concrete manifestation of the gospel mandate to love both God and neighbor. The prophet Micah expressed it best: "What is good has been explained to you, man; this is what Yahweh asks of you: only this, to act justly, to love tenderly and to walk humbly with your God" (Mic 6:8).

Discussion Questions

1. Should the American bishops be issuing statements on the economy?
2. Do you support the individualist or communitarian perspective on justice?
3. Cite instances of social injustice in your local community or state.
4. Which national policies promote social justice? Which do not promote social justice?
5. Is preferential treatment ever justified? If so, under which conditions would it be justified?

Suggested Readings

The statement by the American bishops is *Economic Justice for All* (Washington, D.C.: United States Catholic Conference, 1986). Most scholars regard Pope Leo XIII's encyclical *Rerum Novarum* (*On the Condition of Workers*) in 1891 as the beginning of modern papal social teaching. *Rerum Novarum* is reprinted in *Contemporary Catholic Social*

Teaching (Washington, D.C.: United States Catholic Conference, 1991). In 1991 the encyclical Centesimus Annus *(On the Hundredth Anniversary of Rerum Novarum)* was issued by Pope John Paul II (Washington, D.C.: United States Catholic Conference, 1991). See also the encyclical *Sollicitudo Rei Socialis (On Social Concern)* by Pope John Paul II (Washington, D.C.: United States Catholic Conference, 1987). For a summary of the key documents in this tradition, see chapter three of *Doing Faithjustice: An Introduction to Catholic Social Thought* by Fred Kammer, S.J. (Mahwah: Paulist, 1991). During recent past presidential elections, the administrative board of the United States Catholic Conference has issued a statement in which the board discusses the role of the church in the political order and outlines the church's stance on a number of key social issues. See *Political Responsibility: Revitalizing American Democracy* (Washington, D.C.: United States Catholic Conference, 1991).

Two helpful anthologies are available to students, both edited by David J. O'Brien and Thomas A. Shannon. See *Renewing the Earth: Catholic Documents on Peace, Justice and Liberation* (Garden City: Image Books, 1977) and *Catholic Social Thought: The Documentary Heritage* (Maryknoll: Orbis, 1992). See also Joseph Gremillion's *The Gospel of Peace and Justice* (Maryknoll: Orbis, 1976). A solid introduction to the theories of justice can be found in *Six Theories of Justice* by Karen Lebacqz (Minneapolis: Augsburg, 1986).

Helpful case studies can be found in *Christian Ethics: A Case Method Approach*, edited by Robert Stivers, et al. (Maryknoll: Orbis, 1989).

Euthanasia

Discuss the following cases. Was the action justified or unjustified?

1. A twenty-five year old woman is suffering from inoperable, incurable brain cancer. She has been suffering a great deal of pain despite receiving a high level of pain-killing medication. Her physician has known her since her teens, when she was actively involved in her high school sports program. She later excelled in many sports in her college career. After graduation her coordination skills gradually diminished and she was diagnosed as having cancer when she was twenty-three. She begs her physician to "please let me go." The physician writes her a prescription for fifty painkiller tablets and says, "Be sure not to take twenty pills—that would kill you." The woman dies the following week of an overdose of painkillers.[1]

2. An elderly woman is admitted to a hospital in an unconscious state after suffering a stroke. The woman has suffered little ill health throughout her life and has never, to the best recollection of her loved ones, expressed any opinions or wishes regarding life sustaining procedures. The long term effects of the stroke are at this time

impossible to determine. The family requests that she not be revived if she were to go into cardiac arrest.

3. An elderly couple has no children and only distant relatives. The husband has suffered from Alzheimer's disease for nearly fifteen years and no longer recognizes his wife. The health of his wife who is the sole care-giver has recently begun to fail and she worries about who would care for her husband should she predecease him. Feeling that she would "never have her real husband back again" she suffocates her sleeping husband with a pillow and immediately calls the police to confess.

4. A married thirty year old member of an emergency medical team crew in a large city is accustomed to seeing great human tragedy and misery. He informs his close friends and relatives that if he should ever lapse into a permanent coma he would want them to "pull the plug" on him. He suffers a serious head injury in an automobile accident and the doctors estimate his chance at regaining consciousness at less than 1%. His injury has not, however, affected his body's ability to breathe or regulate any essential bodily functions. With the permission of his wife, a feeding tube is inserted into his stomach through the abdominal wall. After two years there are still no indications that the patient will regain consciousness. His wife petitions the hospital to remove the feeding tube. The hospital ethics committee refuses the request.

5. A young boy is suffering from an incurable disease that progressively diminishes his ability to breathe. Procedures can be performed to ease temporarily the patient's labored breathing, but the relief does not retard the steady progression of the disease. As the disease progresses, the trips to the hospital for emergency

treatment become more frequent. The mother finally asks the medical staff not to treat her son, but simply "give him something for his pain, and let him die." The doctors comply with the mother's requests.[2]

6. An anencephalic baby does not possess a fully developed brain; in most cases only the brain stem has developed. However, the brain stem does control the involuntary bodily functions such as respiration and heart rate. A couple decides to allow their anencephalic baby to be a heart donor for another baby. The problem is that if they wait until the donor dies, carbon dioxide will build up in the tissue and reduce the chances for success in the organ transplant. The couple decides to have the baby's heart removed before the baby dies.

7. A child is born with Down's Syndrome and a number of physical deformities. The child has a deformed esophagus that prevents normal swallowing. The condition can be remedied with a relatively easy procedure of corrective surgery. If the operation is not performed the child will not survive. The family requests that the operation not be performed.

The current medical technology that enables us to do so much good for so many people also scares most of us. While this technology often saves our lives, it also occasionally extends it in ways that many people find frightful and, in some cases, unnecessary. The discussion of euthanasia forces us to make decisions about the appropriate and inappropriate use of this technology. On a deeper level, the discussion of euthanasia forces us to confront the fragility of the human condition. Many of us will experience serious illness; all of us will die. In this discussion, therefore, we are literally dealing with questions of life and death. It is helpful, then, to begin with a Christian understanding of human existence.

The Christian understanding of human existence has within it certain creative tensions. On the one hand, Christians believe that all life is a gift from God. As such, all life is precious and must be preserved and respected in accordance with the will of God. Suicide, for example, is a sin because it is ultimately not our right to take the life God has given to us. The sanctity of human life compels us to come to the assistance of those whose lives are threatened by disease. For example, it would be foolish not to tend to a life-threatening wound in the belief that if the person died, he or she would be at peace in heaven. On the other hand, life on this earth is of a limited duration. In our allotted years we are to do the will of the creator, but there will come a time when we will die, and we have the faithful assurance that in our death the Lord will not abandon us. Christian faith neither regards death itself as evil in all cases nor sees death as having the final word. For these reasons, death need not be prevented at all costs in all cases. Both of these considerations—that life is precious, but that it need not be preserved by every means possible at all times—call us to steer a course between needless prolongation of life on the one hand and not exercising appropriate care of our fellow human beings on the other. Working out the appropriate response in each specific situation is indeed a difficult task, but some important distinctions employed by ethicists may provide some degree of guidance as one approaches specific cases.

Distinctions in the Euthanasia Debate

Ethicists are fond of making distinctions, but such distinctions are not without their purpose. This is true, for example, in the difference between self-defense and murder.

In both cases human life is taken, but the conditions in which the taking of human life occurs makes all the moral difference in the world. The most basic distinction underlying the euthanasia debate is between "allowing someone to die" and "killing someone." This reflects the tension in the Christian tradition regarding life as a gift to be cherished, but ultimately surrendered. It would follow from this understanding that "killing someone" would be wrong, while "allowing someone to die" would be acceptable. Such distinctions are often easier to make in theory than in practice.

Other relevant distinctions are drawn in this debate, but we will confine our consideration to three of the most important ones.

First, we need to consider the question, "Who makes the decision to end life-sustaining treatment?" The wishes of the patient are ethically relevant in these matters. One patient may have strong objections about the use of life-sustaining technology and may have completed an "advance directive" or "living will" which contains detailed instructions regarding the use of such technology; another patient may wish to sustain life for as long as possible. A third patient may have never expressed a concern in either direction. Should someone fall into a medical condition in which decisions must be made about the use of life-sustaining technology, someone must make the final determination about the use of life-sustaining treatment. In essence, the possibilities boil down to two. Either the patient's stated wishes are followed or someone acting on behalf of that patient makes the crucial decisions. If the patient's wishes have been made known and those directives are followed and death results, this is an act of voluntary euthanasia. If someone other than the patient must make that decision and death results, this is an act of compulsory euthanasia.[3]

The second question is, "How does death result?" Here we enter into the thorny issue of what constitutes "playing

God" and what constitutes a responsible exercise of beneficence. There is a common, though not unchallenged, distinction between withholding treatment that would prolong life and performing actions intended to end a life. The theological issue question here is: Which actions are in keeping with the belief that God alone gives and takes life? It is the difference between "letting the disease take its course" and "killing someone." If life-sustaining treatment is withheld and death results we describe this as an act of indirect or passive euthanasia. If the physician gives a patient a lethal injection and death is intended, we describe this act as direct or active euthanasia. The focal point here is the distinction between responsible and irresponsible involvement in bringing about the end of human life.

The third distinction involves the medical technology itself. "What type of treatment or care is required to be given or accepted?" The U.S. bishops repeat the official teaching: "One is not obliged to use either 'extraordinary' means or 'disproportionate' means of preserving life—that is, means which are understood as offering no reasonable hope of benefit or as involving excessive burdens."[4] The determination of whether a treatment is "ordinary" or "proportionate" versus "extraordinary" or "disproportionate" involves weighing "the type of treatment to be used, its degree of complexity or risk, its cost and the possibilities of using it" against "the result that can be expected, taking into account the state of the sick person and his or her physical and moral resources."[5] Ordinary means of life-support offer patients a reasonable hope of recovery without serious expense or inconvenience (e.g., an otherwise healthy patient receives an I.V. to fight a viral infection). Thomas Shannon clarifies the meaning of these categories, "A treatment's routine or customary use in the practice of medicine or even its being lifesaving does not make such a treatment morally ordinary. One must look to the benefits and burdens to see if there is a disproportion."[6] This avoids, according to Shannon, "an equivocation between what is medically ordinary—meaning routine—and what is morally ordinary—meaning a favorable proportion of benefits to burdens."[7]

There is one final area of clarification we need to consider. This concerns the commonly used expression of "brain death." News reports are filled with accounts of people who have suffered serious injury in an automobile accident or shooting and are declared "brain dead." This expression, however, can refer to different physical conditions. The concept of "brain death" itself has arisen as states have attempted to determine the point at which a person is legally dead. Some states defined death as the cessation of breathing or heart rate. The definition, however, gradually shifted from the activity of the lungs or heart to that of the brain. The brain, however, is comprised of different sections. In very general terms, the brain stem controls involuntary bodily functions such as respiration and heart rate. The cerebrum controls the "higher powers" of the brain such as creative thought and interaction with the environment. Patients may suffer injuries to their cerebrum, but incur no damage to their brain stems. This is the basis for two understandings of "brain death." In 1968 a committee at the Harvard Medical School set out to determine reliable criteria by which to measure death. They arrived at four criteria: unreceptivity and unresponsitivity, no movements or breathing, no reflexes, and a flat EEG. All four tests should be repeated after twenty-four hours, since in cases of certain drug overdoses or hypothermia (body temperature below 90 degrees F), brain activity may be so deeply suppressed that it would not register on the EEG.[8] The Harvard criteria measure the activity of the *entire* brain, and consequentially a patient who fails to meet any of the criteria set out by the Harvard definition is legally dead. This is "whole brain death." All parts of the brain have ceased to function. In contrast to this, the second type of "brain death" refers to the situation when the patient's cerebrum has been irreparably damaged, but the brain stem remains intact. This patient is said to be in a "persistent vegetative state" (PVS). This is "cerebral brain death." This patient will not regain consciousness but is able to survive physically if given food and hydration through a feeding tube.

The concept of "brain death" looks to a bodily organ (i.e., the brain) to determine the point at which the patient is legally dead. Some do not equate the concept of death with any bodily state. Rather, they view death in terms of the quality of life of the patient. This parallels the discussion of "quality of life" in the abortion debate. "Life" is defined in terms of an individual's possession of certain essential qualities that make his or her life truly "human." This includes any number of activities included in our conscious engagement with the world and those closest to us. These "higher" functions of the brain, however, require a healthy cerebrum. If a patient no longer has the capacity to consciously relate with his or her environment, then in a "quality of life" perspective, this patient is "as good as dead."

Is Direct Euthanasia Ever Justified?

This discussion of how to define death has important implications for the euthanasia debate. Let us consider the following question: Is direct euthanasia ever justified?[9] One school of thought looks at the consequences of allowing the direct termination of life in some cases as a positive thing. In doing so, the pain and anguish of the patient is relieved, the family's misery is lifted, and we allow patients to die with dignity rather than suffer the horrible torments of the final stages of the often lingering death process. A second school of thought looks at the consequences and sees mostly negative results. Chief among these negative results is the effect this will have on the society's views toward those who are "burdensome." Treating the sick can often place a great deal of emotional and financial stress on a family, but their condition can present for both the dying and those who care for them an opportunity to learn Christian compassion and perhaps experience a deeper understanding of life and the mysteries of the Christian faith. Direct euthanasia reduces those who need our care to burdens or obstacles, and allowing direct euthanasia would make us less compassionate and caring about human life.[10] The third school of thought would categorically oppose any direct assault on innocent human life. No consideration is given here to consequences; the matter is simply not negotiable in any way. The Vatican Declaration states emphatically, "It is necessary to state firmly once more that nothing and no one can in any way permit the killing of an innocent human being, whether a fetus or an embryo, an infant or an adult, an old person, or one suffering from an incurable disease, or a person who is dying."[11]

Feeding Tubes

One of the most controversial issues to arise in this debate is the question of whether it is morally permissible to remove a feeding tube from a permanently comatose patient. Commonly inserted through the nasal passage or directly into the stomach, feeding tubes provide food and hydration to patients. Before such technology, patients would die of starvation or pneumonia. Now they are able to survive for decades. In one case, Paul Brophy, a firefighter, suffered the rupture of an aneurysm and became permanently uncon-scious.[12] A feeding tube was inserted through the abdominal wall into his stomach. The chances for Mr. Brophy's recovery were virtually nil. Given his occupation, Mr. Brophy frequently witnessed great human suffering and disability. He spoke openly of his desire not to be put on a life support system. His wife requested that the feeding tube be removed. A legal battle ensued. The courts eventually ruled that the feeding tube should be removed. Mr. Brophy died eight days after the feeding tube was removed. The distinctions we drew earlier now come into play. What weight should be given to the expressed wishes of Mr. Brophy that he not be put on a life support system? Is the removal of a feeding tube an act of direct or indirect euthanasia? Is a feeding tube an ordinary or extraordinary means of life support? Such determinations, as noted above, require a weighing of the burdens and benefits experienced by the patient. Some see providing food and water as ordinary medical care that results in the prolongation of human life. Despite the burdens to both the patient and the family, the care must be continued. Others regard the feeding tube as a form of extraordinary medical technology that provides no benefit to a patient who is permanently comatose. The technology, it is argued, brings about an effect (i.e., the prolongation of life), but not a benefit.[13] Feeding tubes may, therefore, be removed. Both parties accept as valid the distinction between "ordinary" and "extraordinary" care, but they differ in how to apply that distinction to the specific issue of the removal of feeding tubes. Finally, what role do "quality of life" considerations play in the decision to remove or not remove the feeding tube?

Medical technology seems to echo that ancient pre-occupation with fire: we are attracted and repelled by it at the same time. We want the latest medical technology made available to us as quickly as it is possible to deliver it. Yet, we fear at some point we will become enslaved by our own technological creations. Complicating this further is the

Christian affirmation that life is a precious gift which must be protected and cherished, but which ultimately must be surrendered. Christians confronted with making the decisions regarding the care and treatment of their loved ones or themselves face a painful, difficult, and weighty challenge since they are literally dealing with a matter of life and death.

Discussion Questions

1. Is there any real difference between direct and indirect euthanasia?
2. Is direct euthanasia ever ethically justified?
3. Is it unethical to refuse all medical treatment?
4. Could a feeding tube ethically be removed?
5. What does Christian faith add to this discussion?

Suggested Readings

The official church position can be found in the *Declaration on Euthanasia* issued by the Congregation for the Doctrine of the Faith (Washington, D.C.: United States Catholic Conference, 1980). The Committee for Pro-Life Activities of the National Conference of Catholic Bishops issued *Nutrition and Hydration: Moral and Pastoral Reflections* (Washington, D.C.: United States Catholic Conference, 1992).

Students should see *What Are They Saying About Euthanasia?* by Richard M. Gula, S.S. (Mahwah: Paulist, 1986) for a very helpful overview of the major positions involved in this debate. See also *Mercy or Murder?: Euthanasia, Morality and Public Policy*, edited by Kenneth R. Overberg, S.J. (Kansas City: Sheed and Ward, 1993) and *Hard Decisions: Forgoing and Withdrawing Artificial Nutrition and Hydration* by Eileen P. Flynn (Kansas City: Sheed and Ward, 1990). See also Richard A. McCormick, S.J., "Nutrition-Hydration: The New Euthanasia?" in *The Critical Calling: Reflections on Moral*

Dilemmas Since Vatican II (Washington, D.C.: Georgetown University Press, 1989), chapter twenty-one. *Commonweal* published a supplement in its August 9, 1991 issue (pp. 465–480) dealing with a proposed initiative in the state of Washington to legalize active euthanasia.

War

Would the following be justified? Why? Why not?

1. A group of soldiers on patrol are able by an amazing bit of luck to capture a high-ranking military officer of the opposing forces. Through military intelligence it has been learned that the enemy is planning to launch several key offensives in the area, but the specific details are not known. The captured officer refuses to make any comments. The commanding officer steps forward and begins to torture the prisoner in order to gain information about the exact details of the planned offensives which will most likely be aimed directly at his soldiers.

2. A young Christian man receives a draft notice during the Vietnam war. While he admits that he is scared about the possibility of going to Vietnam, he feels that deep in his heart this particular cause is unjust and he applies for "conscientious objector" status. His request is approved and he serves in the military assisting in military hospitals. He never carries a weapon.

3. A young man enlists in the army. Army intelligence believes that a small town is the center of enemy opposition. The young soldier is informed that those in the town

are believed to be either actively involved in the effort to attack his side or are sympathetic to that cause and often hide enemy soldiers. The order is given to destroy the town. When they land by helicopter, the troops receive no enemy fire and the town appears to be relatively calm, occupied with only women and children. Soldiers begin to shoot the citizens. The young man refuses to fire upon the people.

4. A corrupt dictator has been in power for ten years. There is widespread disenchantment with the dictator on the part of the people, but opposition party leaders are constantly threatened and some have died under suspicious circumstances. In order to maintain lucrative trade agreements with the country's allies, the dictator orders an election. To no one's surprise, the dictator is "elected" as president in a fraudulent election, though observers have no direct evidence of tampering with the ballots. The "elected" president declares that his first order of business is to rid the country of "subversives." A group of students from the university ban together and plot to kill the official president of the country.

5. A nation stockpiles large quantities of chemical and biological weapons. This nation's leaders insist they would never use such weapons, but contend that the arsenal serves as a powerful deterrent to other countries' aggression.

6. A nation's leaders attack a neighboring region, which has long been a subject of territorial dispute, and begin to engage in massive human rights violations. The president of the United States is under pressure to intervene. Such intervention would require a military commitment beyond what the American public would support.

Believing the resolution of the conflict does not directly affect America's national security, the president refuses to commit any sizable number of U.S. troops to the UN peace-keeping forces in the region. The human rights abuses continue.

7. A small patrol comprised of members of an elite corps of American and British soldiers during World War II penetrates enemy lines and moves into a major manufacturing city in Germany. Their mission is to gather certain information about the manufacturing plants in that city and return to the Allied side before dawn. Spotting a Nazi patrol, this group quietly enters what they believe to be a vacant house. To their surprise a family is sleeping in that building. A five year old boy suddenly awakes and begins to scream when he sees the soldiers. Fearing the boy's screams will attract the attention of the Nazi patrol, one of the Allied soldiers kills the boy.

8. United States troops are part of a UN peace-keeping force whose mandate is to secure the stability of food transport lines through a country torn by a civil war which further worsens the living conditions there. Outside the major cities there is massive starvation. The original mandate of the UN troops was to be "peace keepers," but factional leaders within that country begin to order their loyalists to set land mines and attack UN forces with sniper fire. Leaders in the UN do not wish to be perceived as "imperialists" invading a small country, so they do not allow the UN troops to fire on any targets "unless first fired upon." Feeling frustrated by their inability to strike out against their attackers, lower ranking officers order and carry out raids on the headquarters of leaders of the factions believed responsible for the land mines and snipers.

9. **A developing nation is surrounded by nations closely aligned with a religious faction that seeks its annihilation. The developing country has invested a great deal of revenue into its nuclear arms program in the hope that such a military capability will deter the surrounding nations from attacking it. Tension in the region increases and finally a minor incident results in a declaration of war against the developing nation. Using conventional weapons, the neighboring nations attack and win crucial battles easily. Reports of slaughters of entire towns and villages reach the capital city. As enemy troops move toward the capital, the developing nation fires nuclear warheads at key sites in the adjoining countries.**

Christians who turn to the New Testament for moral guidance often feel discouraged when they discover that Jesus issued very few specific moral prohibitions. Jesus did, however, make a number of very specific comments regarding one issue: violence. Contained most concisely in the sermon on the mount (Mt 5–7), these sayings have been debated and dissected by Christians down through the centuries. Some Christians have argued that these teachings are to be followed literally at all times; others have virtually ignored them; and still others have interpreted them in such a way that they are neither literally obeyed nor constantly ignored. All three of these responses will be explored. The central question under consideration remains: Is it ever morally permissible for Christians to act violently?

The starting point for this discussion has been, and continues to be, the sermon on the mount. In the sermon Jesus first cites what has been previously taught and follows that with his own teaching regarding that matter. Jesus' teachings follow a certain pattern: "You have heard it was said....But I say to you...." For example, Jesus cites the known prohibition against adultery, but then elevates the challenge by turning to the interior of the human heart (cf. Mt 5:27–30). "You have heard it was said, 'You shall not commit adultery.' But I say to you, everyone who looks at a woman with lust has already committed adultery with her in his heart." Jesus "radicalizes" the demand in the sense that he goes to the root of the problem. Not committing adultery is good, but it is not sufficient for holiness. Holiness resides not simply in one's ability to overcome evil desires (important and praiseworthy as that is), but in one's inner disposition to want nothing but to do God's will.

The teachings in the sermon on the mount regarding violence follow the same pattern. "You have heard that it was said, 'An eye for an eye and a tooth for a tooth.' But I say to you, offer no resistance to one who is evil" (Mt 5:38–39a). Later the same pattern recurs. "You have heard that it was said, 'You shall love your neighbor and hate your enemy.' But I say to you, love your enemies, and pray for those who persecute you, that you may be children of your heavenly Father, for he makes his sun rise on the bad and the good, and causes rain to fall on the just and the unjust" (Mt 5:43–45). The critical question for Christians is: How do we interpret such verses?

We will examine three conclusions reached by Christians. The first, pacifism, regards the teachings of Jesus as absolutely binding on all Christians. Therefore, Christian participation in any warfare is always immoral. The second conclusion, Christian militarism, places such admonitions in the wider context of the advancement of the Christian cause. Supporters draw upon those biblical passages which not only allow war, but in fact encourage those engaged in a holy cause to pursue such an endeavor with great zeal. For example, in the story of the conquest of the promised land, Joshua is commanded by God to kill all living creatures, including women and children, old and young, and all animals (cf. Jos 6). The third conclusion, known as the just war position, steers a middle course between pacifism and militarism. Unlike pacifism, the just war position does allow for Christian participation in limited violence under certain circumstances. Unlike militarism, restraint is still required and ethical boundaries are maintained. All three of these require further elaboration.

The pacifists' position begins with one specific concern: How should *Christians* live their lives? Since Christians regard Christ as the norm of their morality, their ethical conclusions should follow directly from what Jesus said and did during his ministry. First, Jesus commands us to love our enemies in starkly unambiguous terms. The gospel writers use the Greek word "agape" when relating Jesus' love commands. "Agape" refers to the love of a parent to a child. God loves us as a parent loves a child; therefore we should love one another as our brothers and sisters. Second, Jesus' actions embodied this love. Even at his death, he demonstrated his commitment to a life of agape. John Howard Yoder, a leading Christian pacifist, notes:

> Christ is agape; self-giving, nonresistant love....At the cross this nonresistance, including the refusal to use political means of self-defense, found its ultimate revelation in the uncomplaining and forgiving death of the innocent at the hands of the guilty. This death reveals how God deals with evil; here is the only valid starting point for Christian pacifism or nonresistance. The cross is the extreme demonstration that agape seeks neither effectiveness nor justice, and is willing to suffer any loss or seeming defeat for the sake of obedience.[1]

Yoder reminds us that the death of Christ is not the final chapter in the gospel story.

Yoder insists that Christian pacifism is not rooted in human sentimentality about the goodness of all humans or in some vague trust that "everything will work out in the end." Rather, Christians base their hope in the conviction that the Father did not allow injustice to have the final word. Yoder continues, "But the cross is not the defeat. Christ's obedience unto death was crowned by the miracle of the resurrection and the exaltation at the right hand of God....Effectiveness and success had been sacrificed for the sake of love, but this sacrifice was turned by God into a victory....But before the resurrection there was the cross, and the Christian must follow his Master in suffering for the sake of love."[2] Christian pacifists do not commend their position on the basis of human altruism, but rather view non-violence as the only way of life in accordance with what Jesus did and taught while he was among us.

Christian militarism represents the opposite end of the ethical spectrum from pacifism. Though not a position that has received a wide following in Christian circles, it has appeared in various guises throughout Christian history. The crusades are perhaps the clearest, though not the only, example of this school of thought. The historical record indicates that Christians have engaged in various military campaigns that have subordinated all ethical considerations to the one overriding concern: victory. How is such a perspective justified in light of the sermon on the mount? Here psychological and theological forces combine to form an ideology which justifies such behavior on the part of Christians. Lisa Cahill points out that the pivotal psychological move occurs when Christians define a certain group as outsiders who are unworthy of our concern.[3] In this way, the goal, not the means of achieving the goal, becomes the focal point. If the goal can be theologically defended as being in conformity with the will of God (e.g., the recovery of the holy lands during the crusades), then the means by which Christians achieve that goal is not of great moral concern.

Consequently, there are few, if any, rules to be observed when carrying out that divinely willed military campaign.

The just war position attempts to steer a middle course between pacifism and militarism. A brief review of the development of the just war theory illustrates how it evolved as an attempt to mediate competing concerns within the Christian tradition. We have no strong evidence to doubt that the Christians of the first century were pacifists. One may attribute this to any number of causes. Perhaps the teachings of the sermon on the mount were seen as absolutely binding; perhaps they expected the imminent end of the world; perhaps the persecution of the Romans completely quelled any interest in defending the state; or perhaps most Christians were of such a low social standing that military service was not a viable option for them. By the end of the second century we have records of Christians in the military. The decisive event, however, occurred in the third century when the emperor Constantine supported Christianity. This one event represented a total shift in the church's status in the Roman empire. No longer the subject of persecution, the church now enjoyed the support of the state. Defense of the state was now seen as being in the best interest of the church. Less than a century later, the state needed defending against the invasion of the barbarians. This sets the stage for one of the most influential thinkers in the just war tradition.

St. Augustine provides one of the first defenses of the notion of Christian participation in a "just war." Augustine believed that a Christian's love should be "ordered" properly. In modern jargon, Augustine insisted that we "get our priorities straight." We should love God above all, then neighbor, and then self. That is the proper ordering of one's loves. Given this understanding of the Christian life, self-defense was not an acceptable reason for killing one's neighbor since it placed concern for self before that of God and neighbor, even if the neighbor should be an unjust aggressor. Innocent third parties, however, presented a different challenge. Suppose an unjust aggressor is about to harm someone. Here I am not torn over loving my neighbor above myself. Instead, I am torn between my love for my two neighbors. In this case, my love for my innocent neighbor may compel me to act violently to restrain or possibly kill my neighbor who is about to harm an innocent person. In doing so, Augustine concluded, a Christian does not violate the proper ordering of one's loves. This provides one of the first "test cases" for Christian aggression and serves as the starting point for the just war tradition.

This tradition becomes refined over many centuries. It is important to remember, however, that the burden of proof falls on those who would advocate the use of violence. Non-violence is presumed to be the posture of Christians, but cases could be considered in which violence is tolerated. Which conditions would have to exist before a Christian could actively engage in military conflict? The American bishops drew upon centuries of Christian ethical reflection when they offered the following conditions in their 1983 statement *The Challenge of Peace: God's Promise and Our Response*:

1. Just Cause: "War is permissible only to confront a 'real and certain danger.' "[4]
2. Competent Authority: "War must be declared by those with responsibility for public order."
3. Comparative Justice: "Are the values at stake critical enough to override the presumption against war?"
4. Right Intention: "War can be legitimately intended only for...a just cause."
5. Last Resort: "For resort to war to be justified, all peaceful alternatives must have been exhausted."
6. Probability of Success: We must "prevent irrational resort to force or hopeless resistance when the outcome of either will clearly be disproportionate or futile."

  7. Proportionality: "The damage to be inflicted and the
     costs incurred by war must be proportionate to the
     good expected by taking up arms."

The bishops also propose two principles for determining
appropriate and inappropriate action once a war has begun:
proportionality and discrimination. Proportionality means in
short that "Response to aggression must not exceed the
nature of the aggression."[5] Discrimination precludes directly
targeting innocent civilians. "Just response to aggression must
be discriminate; it must be directed against unjust aggressors,
not against innocent people caught up in a war not of their
making."[6]

     A lively exchange continues among the various
participants in this debate. At issue is our understanding of
what it means to be a Christian. Is violent action ever in
keeping with our commitment to the gospel preached by
Jesus? Pacifists obviously argue for the fundamental incom-
patibility between Christian faith and violent action. The
pacifists charge that the just war proponents have committed
a crucial error when they define their commitments as
Christians in terms of their national identities. The pacifists
insist that we are Christians who happen to live in the United
States, not United States citizens who happen to be Christian.
This distinction proves decisive when contemplating the
use of violence. The focus, charge the pacifists, must be on
the gospel, not on the defense of arbitrarily drawn national
boundaries. The parable of the good Samaritan, the pacifists
insist, challenges that nationalistic point of view. Second,
while all killing is morally repugnant to the pacifist, the idea
that one Christian might kill another Christian for any reason
whatsoever strikes the pacifist as completely antithetical to
the understanding of all Christians being brothers and sisters
in the Lord.

     The pacifists also raise a number of practical concerns.

They question the precision of the just war criteria. For example, how do we know we are fighting for a just cause? Is human motivation so pure that we would fight for only one reason? Could we justify our other less altruistic aims under the banner of a noble cause? When have we reached a last resort? Are there means of resolving the conflict which have eluded us? One of the most difficult areas is determining legitimate authority. The American Revolution is a case in point. Americans rejected the claims of their British sovereigns. David Hollenbach writes, "In cases of revolutionary insurrection, where the government has lost its legitimacy through persistent disregard for justice and violation of the human rights of its citizens, this authority may transfer to extra-governmental movements."[7] This statement acknowledges the difficulty one may have identifying the "legitimate authority" at a given moment in time.

Just war theorists charge that pacifists ignore one of the fundamental charges of the gospel: love of neighbor. To allow unjust aggression to continue against an innocent neighbor is simply irresponsible behavior on the part of Christians. If a man were to walk down the street hurling fire bombs into the houses as he walked, the minimal ethical response would be to restrain him from committing further acts of destruction. The fact that force may be required in order to restrain the man does not render that action immoral. Jesus, after all, overturned the tables of the money changers in the temple.

Just war proponents also contend that support for one's country does not necessarily translate into an abandonment of gospel ideals. If one were to support one's government at all times in all places simply because it is one's place of birth, then the pacifists' complaint would be on target. Just war theorists, however, insist that they factor into their consideration the legitimacy of the government that is asking its citizenry to fight on its behalf. They do not, as the pacifists imply, blindly follow their government. Not all governments are established and maintained in the same way; they do not fight for the same causes. Supporting the Allied governments in World War II is, therefore, not the moral equivalent of supporting the Nazi regime. The former upheld the Christian vision of the dignity of all people; the latter did not. Just war theories would conclude that Christian support for the former was justified while support for the latter was not.

The reasoning employed in this debate revolves around the literal teachings of Jesus. Should Christians follow them without exception or is it permissible to weigh those sayings against other concerns? For pacifists, there simply are no overriding concerns. For the just war theorist and the militarist, there are other legitimate concerns that Christians must consider before making a final decision. For the just war proponent, these would include, among other things, the plight of innocent third parties, the cause being defended, or the threat posed by the aggressor to the common good. Interpreters down through the centuries have drawn distinctions that attempt to balance the words of Jesus with the demands of living in the world. Some have argued that the commands of Jesus apply to the state, but not to the individual, or that they apply to the clergy, but not to the laity. Whether these distinctions are valid or not, they raise the thorny question of how those who are called to take up their crosses and follow Christ can live faithfully to the gospel in a world that is often unconcerned with the welfare of the little children Jesus loved so dearly.

Discussion Questions

1. Should Christians always turn the other cheek?
2. Should Christians always obey the state?
3. Is it realistic to speak about rules in warfare?

4. Should Christian have fought against the Nazis in World War II?
5. Does God control which side wins a war?
6. Could nuclear war ever be justified?
7. Does being a citizen of a country obligate that person to defend the country?

Suggested Readings

The official church teaching regarding war can be found in the pastoral letter on war and peace issued by the National Conference of Catholic Bishops, *The Challenge of Peace: God's Promise and Our Response* (Washington, D.C.: United States Catholic Conference, 1983). See also part two, chapter five of the Vatican II constitution *Gaudium et spes* ("Pastoral Constitution on the Church in the Modern World") in *Documents of Vatican II* (Grand Rapids: William B. Eerdmans Publishing Company, 1975), edited by Austin P. Flannery.

Students should see *Love Your Enemies: Discipleship, Pacifism, and Just War Theory* (Minneapolis: Fortress Press, 1994) by Lisa Sowle Cahill. Shorter explorations can be found in *What Are They Saying About Peace and War?* (Mahwah: Paulist Press, 1983) by Thomas A. Shannon, and *War: A Primer for Christians* by Joseph L. Allen (Nashville: Abingdon Press, 1991). For a book-length defense of Christian pacifism, see John Howard Yoder *The Politics of Jesus* (Grand Rapids: Eerdmans Publishing, 1972). See also Yoder's shorter work *What Would You Do?* (Scottdale: Herald Press, 1983).

Capital Punishment

Would you support capital punishment in any of the following cases?

1. A serial killer admits to murdering eight college women over the course of four years. Using his shrewdness and good looks, he is able to gain the confidence of his victims. While on dates with these women, he strangles them and buries their bodies. After each murder, he moves quickly to another part of the country. After a few months have passed, he repeats his crime.

2. A twenty-five year old man with the mental age of a seven year old boy kills a neighbor. His lawyers present evidence that he himself was abused as a child and he seems unaware of the seriousness of his crime.

3. A disgruntled employee of a wealthy corporation kidnaps an executive. The employee demands ransom and intends to return the executive safely, but after three days without heart medication the executive suffers a heart attack and dies.

4. A fifteen year old gang member wishes to rise quickly in the ranks of his gang. He learns the habits of a rival gang's leader and offers to kill the rival leader in exchange for a

leadership position in his own gang. His fellow gang members approve and weeks later he kills the leader of the rival gang.

5. A hit man for organized crime admits to carrying out thirty to forty hits. Instead of seeking the death penalty, the district attorney offers a deal in which the hit man gives damaging testimony against the head of the crime family in exchange for receiving a ten year sentence and a new identity when released from prison.

6. A businessman involved in an affair begins to suffer financial difficulty. He mentions to his lover that he has a substantial insurance policy on his wife's life. She mentions to the businessman in passing the name of a man who would execute his wife. After some time, the businessman hires the hitman to kill his wife, but he never mentions this to his lover. The man's wife is killed. Both the man and his lover are later arrested.

7. A fourteen year old boy kills a five year old boy at a camp for emotionally disturbed children. The attorneys argue that the fourteen year old boy's troubles result from a drug his mother took during pregnancy.

8. Believing no one is home, a burglar breaks into a house, but he carries a loaded weapon with him. As he walks upstairs, he hears a noise from an upstairs bedroom. He decides to flee the residence, but trips and his gun discharges, killing a woman behind the bedroom door.

9. An admitted murderer spends ten years in jail awaiting execution. During that time he claims he has had a religious awakening and expresses remorse for his crime.

Would you allow the following?

10. In the next election voters will face a referendum on capital punishment. A local television station requests permission to broadcast an actual execution so that voters will be better informed about the death penalty.

Reports of brutal, senseless violence shock and scare us. On one level, we are appalled by the degree of inhumanity that one person can exhibit against another. On another level, such incidents shatter our sense of security and painfully remind us of our own vulnerability to random attack. These highly charged·responses often make for tense debate when dealing with the issue of capital punishment. Some believe it restores justice or offers some consolation to the victims of violent crimes or their families. Others view the act as barbaric and call for its abolition. For Christians living in the United States, this debate takes place on two fronts. We must first consider the constitutional question involved in this controversy and then evaluate the religious and pragmatic arguments advanced by both proponents and abolitionists.

The Constitutional Question

The U.S. Supreme Court's deliberations on the con-stitutionality of capital punishment center on the Eighth Amendment guarantee against cruel and unusual punishment. In its 1972 decision, *Furman v. Georgia,* the Supreme Court held that the death penalty was at that time being applied in a discriminatory fashion. The court did not rule that capital punishment was itself cruel and unusual, but that its present application (i.e., circa 1972) amounted to a violation of the Eighth Amendment. States that wished to preserve their death penalty statutes began working on revising the process by which a person was sent to death row. In an attempt to comply with the Furman decision, some states made the death penalty mandatory for certain crimes (e.g., first degree murders). This, the states believed, removed the problem of discrimination. Other states instituted a two-step process in which a determination was first made regarding the person's guilt or innocence. If found guilty, the capital offender enters into the second phase of the process in which the appropriate punishment for the crime is determined. This involves weighing aggravating circumstances against mitigating circumstances. Aggravating circumstances increase the heinousness of the crime (e.g., torturing someone before killing the person). Mitigating circumstances reduce the person's responsibility for the act (e.g., diminished mental capacity). The court rejected as unconstitutional the mandatory sentencing, but upheld the two-phase process in its 1976 decision, *Gregg v. Georgia*. Provided that process is in place, the court ruled, states may carry out executions.

The U.S. Bishops' Statement on Capital Punishment

Though the bishops call for the abolition of capital punishment, they acknowledge in their 1980 letter on capital punishment that "Catholic teaching has accepted the principle that the state has the right to take the life of a person guilty of an extremely serious crime, and that the state may take appropriate measures to protect itself and its citizens from grave harm...."[1] This position found expression in the great medieval Catholic theologian Thomas Aquinas. Aquinas placed a great emphasis on the "common good" and envisioned the state playing an important role in maintaining the common good. Since a first-degree murderer represents a direct threat to the well-being of the state, the state may execute such a criminal. Just as a diseased portion of the body may be removed in order to restore health to the body, a capital offender may be executed in order to restore stability to the state.

The bishops begin their statement with a discussion of the purpose of punishment. Why do we as a society punish people? The bishops cite three traditional justifications. In the first view, punishment should aim at the rehabilitation of the criminal. Here punishment is directly tied with future results. For example, if sentencing a youthful offender to a jail term will produce a more hardened criminal, then perhaps some alternative sentence would be more appropriate since it would more likely increase the chances of this youth becoming a responsible member of society. In the second view, punishment should deter others from committing the same crime. Laws should dissuade those in society who are contemplating committing crimes from doing so. In this way, punishment helps protect the well-being and safety of those in the wider society. The third purpose for punishment is retribution. Retribution consists in the "restoration of the order of justice which has been violated by the action of the criminal."[2] Here the concern rests with "balancing the scales of justice." A criminal violates the "order of justice" and justice demands that the offender pay the price for that violation.

Each of these theories on punishment has its strengths and weaknesses. The goal of rehabilitation is sensible, yet it raises two important questions. First, are all offenders capable of rehabilitation? Second, are there limits to the type of therapy that may be used to produce rehabilitation? Should a violent offender be subjected to shock therapy or surgical operations if it is believed that such procedures could significantly reduce that person's chances of committing future crimes? The goal of deterrence is equally reasonable, but one wonders what deterrent effect laws have on those acting irrationally. This approach also seems uninterested in the issue of proportionality. If jaywalking were to become a capital offense, the incidents of jaywalking would most likely be reduced, but that does not deal with the issue of proportionality between the crime committed and the punishment assigned to the offense. The theory of retribution is praiseworthy for its impartiality. In this theory, justice is truly blind. No matter what the social standing of the offender, all people committing a certain offense receive the same sentence. While this avoids favoritism in the administration of justice, one wonders whether that approach is blind to the particular circumstances of each individual case. Is stealing bread in order to survive the same as stealing for the thrill of it? In other words, does mercy need to temper justice in certain cases?

The bishops maintain that the gospel values are best preserved when we do not support the death penalty. They cite four reasons. First, this refusal to support the death penalty sends a message that we are willing to break the cycle of violence. Second, it respects the dignity of each and every individual. Third, it acknowledges that God alone is the Lord of life. Fourth, it is most consonant with the example of Jesus who taught and practiced forgiveness.[3] Other Christians have advanced arguments in support of the death penalty. Some of their arguments are theological, others are more pragmatic. Of the many arguments on both sides, seven will be discussed.

The Capital Punishment Debate

Issue #1: The Right to Life

Is the right to life absolute or can it be forfeited? This may be a rather abstract question, but it has a direct bearing on the question of capital punishment. On the one hand, some argue that "only God can take a life." In this view, when we execute criminals we are overstepping the moral boundaries established by God. Critics disagree. They charge that those who claim that "only God can take a life" would have to oppose not only capital punishment and abortion, but also all participation in war and even self-defense. Supporters of capital punishment insist that we must distinguish between human activity that takes innocent human life and state-sanctioned activity that takes the lives of capital offenders. The former behavior is immoral while the latter is acceptable since capital offenders have forfeited their right to life by their actions. To use a mundane example, if one acts irresponsibly in a movie theater, one surrenders his or her right to watch the movie. If that person's behavior makes it nearly impossible for the other patrons to enjoy the movie, then that person will be escorted out of the theater. In the same way, those who show utter disregard for the welfare of their neighbors forfeit their right to live in community with them. Those opposing capital punishment would argue that such a stance justifies only the practice of life imprisonment, not actual executions.

Issue #2: Justice

What is just punishment for capital offenders? Those who favor capital punishment typically favor a retribution position. If someone takes a life, then, in the name of justice, that person's life should be taken. Supporters often refer to the story of Noah's covenant with God in which God declares, "If anyone sheds the blood of man, by man shall his blood be shed; For in the image of God has man been made" (Gn 9:6). Opponents of capital punishment assert that supporters of the death penalty frequently confuse justice with vengeance.[4] The execution of capital offenders accomplishes nothing that we as a society would not achieve with life imprisonment, except that it satisfies a deep desire for vengeance against the wrongdoer. Second, opponents of the death penalty charge their adversaries with inconsistency. One can not condemn the taking of human life, they insist, and then punish that action by doing the very thing that is condemned.

Issue #3: Effect on Society

What message does the death penalty send to our society? Proponents of the death penalty insist that laws reflect societal values. There must be a direct correlation between the severity of the crime and the type of punishment the criminal receives. At the highest point in this scale, the most reprehensible crime must be paired with the severest penalty. Therefore, we must reserve capital punishment for those crimes that offend our most cherished moral codes. In doing so, proponents charge, we send a positive message to society that human life is a precious gift of the highest moral value. Critics see the death penalty sending a different message to society. Mario Cuomo, one of the most vocal critics of the death penalty, argues, "The death penalty tells our children that it is OK to meet violence with violence."[5] Capital punishment, it is argued, contributes to a culture of violence. State-sanctioned executions perpetuate the cycle of violence and disregard other less violent means of conflict resolution. Instead of resorting to the exercise of brute force, we as a society should be challenged to find ways of dealing with violence that call upon our creativity and imagination.

Issue #4: Economics

While ethics is not completely a matter of economics, neither is it completely divorced from economic concerns when the issue is the death penalty. Different people would of course give varying weight to this aspect of the capital punishment debate, but it remains a fixture in the overall discussion. Is it cheaper to execute someone or to sentence that person to life imprisonment? It would seem that execution would be cheaper than providing for a prisoner's housing and food for an extended period of time. Executions, however, are expensive. One 1990 report concludes the following:

> A study of the California system suggested a minimum cost of $500,000 per case (includes all capital cases, not just those executed). One of New York State estimated the cost per capital case at 1.8 million, while a Maryland study figured about $750,000 per case. While introducing life imprisonment without parole would probably require a huge prison construction program, costing about $55,000 per cell, the Bureau of Justice Statistics estimates that it costs $11,302 per inmate to operate a confinement facility (1984 *Census of State Adult Correctional Facilities*, WDC, 1987).
>
> Over a 30–40 year period, this amount would likely be considerably less than the current cost of trying to carry out the death penalty. Supporters of the death penalty, however, point out that, while they advocate proper review of the cases, both the lengthy time and high expense result from innumerable appeals, many over "technicalities" which have little or nothing to do with the question of guilt or innocence, and do little more than jam up the nation's court system. If these "frivolous" appeals were eliminated the procedure would neither take so long nor cost so much.[6]

In this summation, one sees both sides represented. Those who oppose the death penalty point out that the cost of execution exceeds that of life imprisonment, while their critics charge that such costs result from the appeals process. If that appeal could be streamlined, then these costs could be contained.

Issue #5: Deterrence

Does having the death penalty deter others from committing capital offenses? Statistics have been marshaled by both sides to substantiate their claims. Proponents of the death penalty argue that having the death penalty as a genuine, realistic possibility for convicted capital offenders deters those contemplating such acts from committing them. They contend that the lengthy appeals process reduces the deterrent effect of the capital punishment statutes. In any event, if the capital punishment laws have deterred even one potential capital offender from committing a capital offense, then the laws are justified. Critics charge that the death penalty does not deter crime. First, those who kill in a fit of rage are not acting rationally. In those cases, reasoned deliberation about the consequences of one's actions simply does not take place. Second, those who engage in premeditated acts almost always do so under the assumption that they will not get caught. In those cases the deterrent value of the law is also lost.

Issue #6: Inequality

Opponents of the death penalty contend that the process is discriminatory in that the poor and minorities are disproportionately given the death penalty as opposed to life imprisonment. They cite instances such as the following: "Since Georgia adopted its current death-penalty law in 1973, four white men in the Columbus district attorney's office have decided which murders will be prosecuted as capital crimes. To date, 78% of their cases have involved white victims, although blacks are the victims in 65% of the community's homicides. Among the other factors that may create greater sympathy for a white victim or defendant: all four judges in the state superior court, which tries capital cases, are white, and often the juries are all white, although blacks account for 35% of the Columbus population."[7] In addition to racial prejudice, there are a number of reasons why this disparity exists. For example, some prosecutors seek the death penalty with great vigor, others do not. Second, if a poor person is accused of a capital offense, he or she does not have the financial resources to hire a high powered defense team. Often that person is represented by an overburdened public defender.

Supporters of the death penalty point out that this complaint addresses only the *application* of the punishment, not the fairness of the punishment itself. If inequalities exist in how the punishment is administered, these can be corrected. The problem, in other words, rests not in the punishment itself, but in the system responsible for the fair and equitable application of that punishment.[8]

Issue #7: The Future

Supporters and opponents of the death penalty differ as well in their concerns for the future. Supporters emphasize that the death penalty prevents any future crime on the part of the convicted. They cite cases where convicted murderers served their sentence and were released, only to kill again. If the murderer had been executed, the lives of these second victims would have been spared. Opponents have a different concern. They fear that at some point in the future we may discover that the convicted murderer was in fact innocent. They cite cases where new evidence has come to light or new ways of testing evidence (e.g., "DNA fingerprinting") have been developed that exonerate a person already put to death. This possibility for error distresses the bishops. They write, "Because death terminates the possibilities of conversion and growth and support that we share with each other, we regard a mistaken infliction of the death penalty with a special horror, even while we retain our trust in God's loving mercy."[9]

Concluding Thoughts

The bishops' statement acknowledges "that many citizens may believe that capital punishment should be maintained as an integral part of our society's response to the evils of crime, nor is this position incompatible with Catholic tradition."[10] The bishops, however, hope to persuade the faithful on the basis of their demonstration of "the evils associated with capital punishment and the harmony of the abolition of capital punishment with the values of the Gospel."[11] Yet Robert Drinan, S.J. writes, "It is sad to have to conclude that neither the nation's Catholics nor the public at large are heeding the church's condemnation of the death penalty."[12]

This debate promises to continue, yet one of the frontiers that might be explored most profitably concerns the question of consistency. Can one be pro-life in abortion, yet favor capital punishment? Does a commitment to the sanctity of life require opposition across the board to abortion, euthanasia, war, and capital punishment? Is there a legitimate line to be drawn between innocent human life and those who attack innocent human life? If so, does the protection of the former necessarily involve protection of the latter? These questions, and many others besides, will fuel the ongoing debate for some time to come.

Discussion Questions

1. Do you support capital punishment? Why? Why not?
2. Respond to the following statement: "Capital punishment is un-Christian."

3. Which argument either for or against capital punishment did you find most compelling and least compelling?
4. If you support capital punishment, what do you regard as the minimum age for execution of a sane capital offender?
5. If you support capital punishment, should we execute capital offenders who are mentally retarded?

Suggested Readings

The official teaching of the United States bishops can be found in their *Statement on Capital Punishment* (Washington, D.C.: United States Catholic Conference, 1980). See also "Capital Punishment and the Sacredness of Life" by Bishop Rene H. Gracida in *Shepherds Speak: American Bishops Confront the Social and Moral Issues That Challenge Christians Today*, chapter eleven, edited by Dennis M. Corrado and James F. Hinchey (New York: Crossroad, 1986). For a collection of statements by religious bodies calling for the abolition of capital punishment, see *The Death Penalty: The Religious Community Calls for Abolition* (Washington, D.C.: National Coalition to Abolish the Death Penalty, 1988).

For contrasting opinions regarding capital punishment, see the essays by Hugo Adam Bedau and Ernest van den Haag in chapter twelve of *Moral Issues and Christian Response*, Fourth Edition, edited by Paul T. Jersild and Dale A. Johnson (Fort Worth: Holt, Rinehart, and Winston, 1988). See also *The Morality of Capital Punishment: Equal Justice Under the Law?* by Michael E. Endres (Mystic: Twenty-Third Publications, 1985). Parish study groups might wish to use *The Death Penalty: A Guide for Christians* by Bob Gross (Elgin: Brethren Press, 1991). An interesting work opposing capital punishment is Dead Man Walking: *An Eyewitness Account of the Death Penalty in the United States* by Helen Prejean, C.S.J. (New York: Random House, 1993).

Notes

Introduction

[1]I will make no distinction between the terms "ethics" and "morality." Both terms in their origins mean "custom." I will also make no distinction between "Christian ethics" and "moral theology." The former expression is more often associated with Protestantism, the latter term with Roman Catholicism.

Reproductive Technology

[1]I am borrowing from Lawrence J. Kaplan and Carolyn M. Kaplan, "Natural Reproduction and Reproduction-Aiding Technologies," in *The Ethics of Reproductive Technology*, edited by Kenneth D. Alpern (Oxford: Oxford University Press, 1992), pp. 23 and 347.

[2]See the article "Artificial Insemination (Moral Aspect)," in the *New Catholic Encyclopedia* (New York: McGraw-Hill, 1967), for the positions in this debate, esp. p. 923.

[3]Some prefer the designation "pre-embryo." See the footnote to the Foreword in the Instruction discussed below.

[4]I am borrowing from Richard McCormick, "Therapy or Tampering? The Ethics of Reproductive Technology," in *America* December 7, 1985, pp. 396–403.

[5]*Instruction on Respect for Human Life in Its Origin and on the Dignity of Procreation: Replies to Certain Questions of the Day* (Washington, D.C.: United States Catholic Conference, 1987). Cf. the *New York Times*, March 10, 1987, for a summary of conclusions which are drawn in the Instruction.

[6]Ibid., p. 24.

[7]According to the Instruction, AIH procedures are to be judged according to the following: "If the technical means facilitates the conjugal act or helps it to reach its natural objectives, it can be morally acceptable. If, on the other hand, the procedure were to replace the conjugal act, it is morally illicit" (p. 32).

[8]See Edward V. Vacek, S.J.'s discussion of the Instruction in "Notes on Moral Theology," esp. pp. 114–120 in *Theological Studies* (49) 1988.

[9]*Instruction*, p. 9.

[10]Archbishop Daniel E. Pilarczyk, "Taking It on the Chin—For Life: Reflections on a Vatican Instruction," *America* 156 (14), April 11, 1987, p. 295.

Abortion

[1]Roe v. Wade in *Biomedical-Ethical Issues: A Digest of Law and Policy Development* (Binghamton: Vail-Ballou Press, 1983), p.15.

[2]Ibid., p. 16.

[3]Many ethicists distinguish between "life" and "personhood." Here I am treating the two terms as synonymous. Later I discuss the positions of those who would argue that personhood does not emerge until some point after conception.

[4]Andrew Varga, S.J., *On Being Human: Principles of Ethics* (New York: Paulist Press, 1978), p. 94.

[5]See Charles E. Curran, chapter eight, "Abortion: Ethical Aspects," in *Transition and Tradition in Moral Theology* (Notre Dame: University of Notre Dame Press, 1979).

[6]Judith Jarvis Thomson, "A Defense of Abortion," reprinted in *The Problem of Abortion*, edited by Joel Feinberg (Belmont: Wadsworth, 1974).

[7]Vincent J. Genovesi, S.J., *In Pursuit of Love: Catholic Morality and Human Sexuality* (Wilmington: Michael Glazier, 1987), p. 345.

[8]The text of Cuomo's speech can be found in *Origins*, September 27, 1984. This address is reprinted in Abortion and Catholicism: The American Debate (see suggested readings).

[9]*Origins* p. 237.

[10]David Carlin, "Abortion, Religion and the Law," *America*, December 1, 1984, p.356.

[11]*Origins* p. 236.

[12]Ibid., p. 238.

Sexual Ethics

[1]*Declaration on Certain Questions Concerning Sexual Ethics* (Washington, D.C.: United States Catholic Conference, 1975), p. 5.

[2]Ibid., p. 6.

[3]Ibid.

[4]Ibid., p. 7.

[5]*Human Sexuality: New Directions in American Catholic Thought* (New York: Paulist, 1977), edited by Anthony Kosnik, et al., p. 82.

[6]Ibid., p. 86.

[7]Ibid., pp. 92–95.

[8]*Letter to the Bishops of the Catholic Church on the Pastoral Care of Homosexual Persons* (Washington, D.C.: United States Catholic Conference, 1986), p. 6.

[9]Ibid., p. 7.

[10]Charles Curran *Transition and Tradition in Moral Theology* (Notre Dame: University of Notre Dame Press, 1979), p. 71.

[11]Peter J. Gomes ,"Homophobic? Re-Read Your Bible," Op-Ed, New York Times, August 17, 1992.

Social Justice

[1]James Sterba, *Morality in Practice*, Second Edition (Belmont: Wadsworth Publishing, 1988), p. 20.

[2]I borrowed this example from Dr. Nancy Duff of Princeton Theological Seminary.

[3]*Economic Justice for All* (Washington, D.C.: United States Catholic Conference, 1986), p. ix.

[4]Ibid.

[5]Ibid., p. 41.

[6]Ibid., p. 40.

[7]Ibid., p. 51.

[8]Ibid., p. 38.

[9]*Brothers and Sisters to Us* (Washington, D.C.: United States Catholic Conference, 1979), p. 3.

Euthanasia

[1]For a case along these lines, see the "Sounding Board" piece by Timothy E. Quill, M.D. in *The New England Journal of Medicine*, March 7, 1991, pp. 691–694. This is reprinted as chapter five in *Mercy or Murder?* (see suggested readings).

[2]Most of the situations presented for discussion here are based on well-known cases. In this case I am borrowing from

An Introduction to Bioethics by Thomas A. Shannon and James J. DiGiacomo (New York: Paulist, 1979), p. 63.

[3]Some do not use the term "compulsory" but rather speak of "non-voluntary" when the patient is not able to say whether treatment should be given or withheld and "involuntary" when the person's requests are known, but not heeded. See Helga Kuhse's "Euthanasia" in *A Companion to Ethics*, edited by Peter Singer (Cambridge: Basil Blackwell, 1991).

[4]"Nutrition and Hydration: Moral and Pastoral Reflections" (Washington, D.C.: United States Catholic Conference, 1992), p. 2.

[5]*Declaration on Euthanasia* (Washington, D.C.: United States Catholic Conference, 1980), p. 3.

[6]Thomas Shannon "How Long Must We Preserve Life?" *America*, December 3, 1993, p. 14.

[7]Ibid.

[8]I am borrowing from Richard Gula, *What Are They Saying About Euthanasia?* (Mahwah: Paulist Press, 1986, p.16).

[9]I am drawing from chapter three of Gula, especially pp. 81–83.

[10]See "Physician-Assisted Suicide: Flight from Compassion" by Richard A. McCormick, S.J. in *The Christian Century*, December 4, 1991, pp. 1132–1134.

[11]*Declaration on Euthanasia*, p. 2.

[12]A very helpful summary of this case can be found in "Should Paul Brophy Have Been Allowed to Die?" by Robert F. Drinan, S.J. in *America*, November 22, 1986.

[13]See Richard McCormick, S.J., " 'Moral Considerations' Ill-Considered," in *America* March 14, 1992, p. 214. See also chapter three of Eileen P. Flynn's *Hard Decisions* (Kansas City: Sheed and Ward, 1990) for a review of the positions in this debate.

War

[1]John Howard Yoder, *The Original Revolution: Essays on Christian Pacifism* (Scottdale: Herald Press, 1977), p. 56.

[2]Ibid., pp. 56–57.

[3]Lisa Sowle Cahill, *Love Your Enemies: Discipleship, Pacifism, and Just War Theory* (Minneapolis: Fortress Press, 1994), chapter seven.

[4]*The Challenge of Peace: God's Promise and Our Response* (Washington, D.C.: United States Catholic Conference, 1983). Quotations relating to each criterion are taken from pp. 28–31.

[5]Ibid., p. 33

[6]Ibid.

[7]David Hollenbach, S.J., *Nuclear Ethics: A Christian Moral Argument* (Mahwah: Paulist Press, 1983), p. 39.

Capital Punishment

[1]U.S. bishops' *Statement on Capital Punishment* (Washington, D.C.: United States Catholic Conference, 1980), p. 3.

[2]Ibid., p. 4.

[3]Ibid., pp. 7–8. For a defense of the bishops' position, see chapter two of *Eight Key Issues in Modern Society: A Catholic Perspective* by Mark Neilsen (Liguori: Liguori Publications, 1990).

[4]See " 'Vengeance is Mine,' Says the Lord," by Richard L. Nygaard in *America*, October 8, 1994, pp. 6–8.

[5]*Time*, April 2, 1990, p. 20.

[6]*Capital Punishment: Cruel and Unusual?* edited by Mark A. Siegel, et al. (Wyllie: Information Plus, 1990), pp. 5–6.

[7]"Race and the Death Penalty" by Jill Smolowe, *Time*, April 29, 1991, pp. 68–69.

[8]See Vincent Barry, *Applying Ethics* (Belmont: Wadsworth,

1985), chapter six, esp., p. 246 for a point-counterpoint discussion along these lines.

[9]U.S. bishops' *Statement on Capital Punishment*, p. 9.

[10]Ibid., p. 12.

[11]Ibid.

[12]Robert Drinan, S.J., "Catholics and the Death Penalty," in *America*, June 18, 1994, p. 14.